Strategy
to Action
in
10 Days

Creating High Performance Organizations

William Seidman, Ph.D.

Michael McCauley

Published by Advantage, Charleston, South Carolina.
Member of Advantage Media Group.

ADVANTAGE is a registered trademark and the Advantage colophon is a trademark of Advantage Media Group, Inc.

Printed in the United States of America.

ISBN: 978-1-59932-166-0
LCCN: 2009912174

This publication is designed to provide accurate and authoritative information in regard to the subject matter covered. It is sold with the understanding that the publisher is not engaged in rendering legal, accounting, or other professional services. If legal advice or other expert assistance is required, the services of a competent professional person should be sought.

Most Advantage Media Group titles are available at special quantity discounts for bulk purchases for sales promotions, premiums, fundraising, and educational use. Special versions or book excerpts can also be created to fit specific needs.

For more information, please write: Special Markets, Advantage Media Group, P.O. Box 272, Charleston, SC 29402 or call 1.866.775.1696.

Visit us online at **advantagefamily**.com

Acknowledgements

As with any book, there are many people to thank for their support. Here are just a few of the people who have helped us along the way. We apologize if we missed anyone.

Heather Ziegler and Jocelyn Burgess believed in us and our approach very early on. They provided us with both their wisdom and an opportunity to experiment. Most important, during some of the early experiments that were less than successful, they stuck with us.

Peter Galen has played a longtime, key role as supporter, board member, and Bill's cousin (so he couldn't get away even if he wanted to). He kept encouraging us, telling us that we would make it, even when times were tight.

Larry Rebich has been our software architect for more than 10 years. Through all the revisions, both to the process and technology, he has continued to create the groundbreaking applications that make our process possible.

Rick Grbavac has made a huge contribution to our work for five years now. As a friend, colleague and confidant, he has enhanced our efforts at every turn. We are indebted to his thoughtful input in the creation of the process and the writing of this book.

Finally, thanks to our families. They have played a huge role in our success. Our sons – David, James, Andrew, Ryan and Darryl – have helped us keep life and work in perspective. Our wives, in a word, are incredible. Johnell McCauley and Elizabeth Lincoln have put up with all of the distractions and conflicts inherent in the creative process. They have held our homes together as we toiled to hold the work together. We love them very much and thank them for their endless support.

Foreword

Strategy to Action in 10 Days

During the last twenty-five years, the theory of transformational leadership has been the most popular approach to understanding and studying outstanding leadership. Research has clearly shown that transformational leaders have more dedicated and satisfied followers, and that together groups and departments led by transformational leaders have higher levels of productivity and performance. Simply put, and as the title of Bernard Bass's 1985 book suggests, transformational leaders lead groups that have levels of "performance beyond expectations."

In their book, Strategy to Action in 10 Days, and in their consulting work with organizations, William Seidman and Michael McCauley have asked and answered the question of whether a research- and science-based technology could be developed that would create the same conditions that make groups led by transformational leaders effective. In other words, regardless of whether a group or department is led by a transformational or non-transformational leader, conditions can be created that help spur the group to high levels of performance, dedication, professionalism, as well as satisfaction with their work and the organization. This is indeed a breakthrough.

I know that some leadership scholars, and many practicing leaders, might find it "heretical" to think that a technology process could substitute for good leadership. But research is clearly showing that leadership in modern organizations is a collective activity. It is not top-down, nor is it purely bottom-up. To be effective, groups and organizations must be thoroughly infused with leadership emanating from all levels of the organization. The technological processes that Bill and Michael lay out in this book will foster good leadership in your organization. It causes all members to engage in leadership, and it makes those in designated leadership positions better leaders.

As a researcher, I am always concerned that leadership strategies, practices, and technologies be solidly grounded in research. In Strategy to Action in 10 Days, Seidman and McCauley have based their methods on both classic and relatively new research on human performance, group processes, and transformational leadership. They have taken this scientific work and fashioned a step-by-step process and accompanying technology to infuse an organization with the best elements of leadership and individual and group processes that will allow an organization to come together, engage members both cognitively and emotionally, and propel them to higher and higher levels of performance.

Perhaps what is most remarkable is how quickly these positive changes can be made in an organization. This is clearly a case where on-line technologies – technologies that can very quickly lead to enormous advancements in processing numbers, information, and ideas – can spur changes in areas that we believe are slow to change: human collective action. While the idea of moving from "strategy to action" in only ten days seems like exaggeration, it is truly remarkable how quickly the implementation of this technology can transform an organization. It is indeed a remarkable breakthrough.

Ronald E. Riggio, Ph.D.
Henry R. Kravis Professor of Leadership
and Organizational Psychology
& Director of the Kravis Leadership Institute
at Claremont McKenna College

Table of Contents

Section 5: Scaling High Performance to Everyone

Section 6: Summing Up

Introduction

Strategy to Action in 10 Days

Everybody has experienced the moment when you've been given a significant "opportunity" that needs to be addressed immediately – preferably yesterday! Many of those opportunities involve improving the performance of your organization by either fixing a problem or preparing the organization for a new requirement. This challenge could be anything from revamping the inventory forecasting process to shortening customer wait time to updating the way insurance agents file claims.

High performance is no longer just a competitive advantage – it's a necessity! And, you need to achieve it fast.

Your personal challenge, should you choose to accept it, is to somehow make your organization into a high-performing entity, fast. You know the coming weeks are going to be rough. Keeping your organization on top in today's competitive business environment requires that everyone, from the janitor to the CEO, operate at the highest levels. High performance is no longer just a competitive advantage – it's a necessity! And, you need to achieve it fast. Is 10 days fast enough?

It Takes Technology to Create Technology

Heather, a manager at one of the nation's largest high- tech manufacturers, was presented with the challenge of managing the "human capabilities" component of a sweeping reorganization of her company's supply chain. If successful, the reorganization was expected to significantly improve customer satisfaction, while generating many millions of dollars in additional profits. Her project would touch almost every portion of the company's supply chain from field sales to factory production. More important it required a change to almost every aspect of these functions. People had to conceive of their jobs differently, adopting new attitudes, developing new skills, and using new business processes and tools. Heather realized that this project would necessitate a profound change to her company's underlying culture. The very future of the company rested on the success of this project. No pressure to succeed here!

Heather had been "around the block" many times and was very well respected for her ability to get things done. She had tried various approaches to similar, though smaller, projects in the past with varying results. For this one, she was convinced that traditional approaches could not achieve what was needed for success. Standard classroom training was out of the question because the "students" were located throughout the world. Flying them all to the home office would be very expensive both in dollars and time lost. In addition, Heather knew that people got very motivated by training, but that motivation wore off just as quickly.

Hiring consultants to go out and coach people in the field was also dismissed because of the prohibitive costs and a lack of uniformity across the company. A management "road show" was also dismissed.

It could be done successfully on a small scale, but trying to conduct sessions throughout the company would require a great deal of time and money.

Heather knew that she needed a different solution. That's when she found us and saw the approach described in this book for the first time. Frankly, Heather was a bit skeptical in the beginning, but she was intrigued enough to try it – and is she ever glad she did!

She began testing with a group in America and then quickly expanded to Europe. The results were excellent. As one senior manager put it:

"You could literally see the difference. People spoke differently to customers and each other, walked with more confidence, and showed enormous excitement. And customer feedback was great too!"

To say that Heather was excited would be an understatement. She then took the system to the Far East and got similar results. Now the testing was complete and it was time for the big program.

The program made a significant, quantifiable and sustainable difference in the way this company worked – worldwide.

She had to develop the forecasting portion of the program and deploy it to 300-plus people in five locations around the world – and do it quickly. She assembled a global team of top performers, gathered their forecasting expertise, and globally deployed the forecasting capability – all in just 10 days! The program had superior best practices, created intense motivation, sustained the behavioral response, and did this for hundreds of people around the world.

The results were excellent. The program made a significant, quantifiable and sustainable difference in the way this company worked – worldwide.

All groups involved report a substantial cultural change, including much-improved forecast accuracy and better relationships with customers. Specific financial metrics (which, for obvious reasons, we are not allowed to share) also show significant improvements.

Heather has succeeded beyond her wildest expectations. If you talk to Heather she will tell you that nothing creates a high-performance organization better or faster than the methodology described here.

It's About More Than Burgers

Kevin, a program manager in the field operations group of one of the nation's largest fast food restaurant companies, had the challenge of implementing numerous change initiatives throughout the company's 1,000-plus restaurants. These initiatives included improvements to restaurant operations such as new kitchen configurations and support for new products, new business processes such as changes to cooking methods and drive-through order management, and development of restaurant and "area coach" team-building skills.

Like Heather, Kevin had tried the usual approaches with decidedly mixed results. Also like Heather, Kevin had a significant challenge in a new, sweeping initiative that was the central element of a multistage program to improve performance. One of the key elements in the initiative was the ability of district managers to educate and guide restaurant managers to develop great restaurant teams.

Anyone who has worked in the fast-food industry knows just how difficult this can be. Few of the 180 district managers had much management training, and there were hardly any programs or systems to support their role. Kevin knew that implementing this initiative was going to require a significant change to the company's culture, as well as to its operational processes.

That's when Kevin discovered us and the process described in this book.

Like Heather, he was skeptical. His company had a very strong culture, with major emphasis on metrics and data, mostly designed to promote short-term performance. But Kevin saw the promise of an approach like ours and decided to move ahead with a test.

Kevin and his team began the test with four restaurants in the Portland, Oregon, area. The initial results surprised even us. After a two-month trial, Kevin's company achieved a sales improvement beyond its hopes. In fact, it calculated that the additional sales were sufficient to pay off the entire investment in our program – in just the first four weeks! The methodology had passed the first hurdle with flying colors.

Kevin expanded the program to the Las Vegas area. The results were similar, showing both an increase in restaurant morale and a decrease in employee turnover (a significant issue in the fast-food industry) along with the increase in sales.

Following those successes the program has been expanded several times, both in scope and geographic area.

Kevin was thrilled. In the face of almost constant resistance, he used this program to guide his company into a new and significantly more profitable approach to business management. Kevin's managers and the company's executives were thrilled too.

Using this approach, you can go from articulating your strategy to implementing it in as little as two business weeks.

If you talk with Kevin about his experience, he will tell you that nothing works better than this methodology for creating a high-performance organization.

So What's New?

The methodology described in this book optimizes organizational performance by giving you the capability to define and deploy innovative best practices faster and more completely than ever thought possible. By "faster," we mean it will take just 10 days from the time you seriously begin to build a set of best practices that will provide the desired performance improvement to the time you can deploy them and see an initial attitudinal and behavioral change. That's right, using this approach, you can go from articulating your strategy to implementing it in as little as two business weeks (Figure 1).

As such, this is a process designed for today's highly volatile and competitive environment.

Traditional approaches are too slow to keep up with the pace of today's business environment, only marginally effective in producing short-term learning, and almost completely ineffective at driving sustained change. This is particularly true when the change must be scaled to hundreds or thousands of people at once.

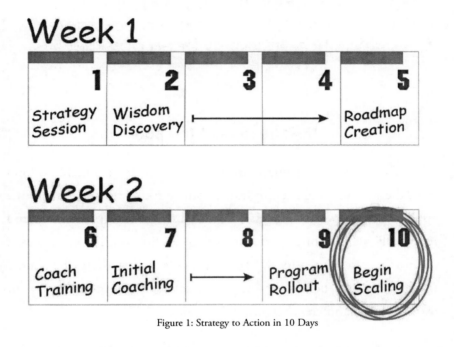

Figure 1: Strategy to Action in 10 Days

How is it possible to go from strategy to action in just 10 days? The approach described here differs from traditional approaches in several significant ways:

- It relies on science, particularly the studies of human brain function (neuroscience), which are constantly breaking new ground in understanding how people learn.

- It relies on a technology called "persuasive technology," which was developed only a few years ago.

- It is a unique combination of four areas of science, including positive deviance, fair process, the previously mentioned neuroscience, and mass customization.

The scientific foundation is critical because it makes the entire process faster, more complete and more predictable than has previously been possible.

The Structure of This Book

This book is organized into sections, each of which explores both the concepts required to frame your thinking for success and the application of specific processes required for you to predictably and repeatedly achieve high performance. In addition, a list of resources is provided in Appendix A. Those provide you with further, more in-depth reading, helping you apply the concepts and processes to your own situation and creating immediate value for you.

Understanding the process itself and the underlying scientific foundation is the focus of Section 1. The scientific foundation is critical because it makes the entire process faster, more complete and more predictable than has previously been possible.

However, this is a more conceptual section that some of you may want to skip. If you do, please keep in mind that everything in the later sections is grounded in very solid research.

How to "set the bar" for high performance is the focus of Section 2. We provide you with a quick way to use the Theory of Positive

Deviance to leverage the wisdom of your most respected internal experts and create the foundation for performance improvement. We provide you with a clear process for identifying your positive deviants and "discovering" their inner wisdom.

Motivating high performance is the focus of Section 3. We provide a proven method for getting people interested in adopting the changes you propose – so interested that they will almost beg you to involve them.

We provide a proven method for getting people interested in adopting the changes you propose – so interested that they will almost beg you to involve them.

Sustaining high performance is the focus of Section 4. We provide a proven method for reinforcing learned behaviors requiring just a few minutes per week.

Scaling the high performance initiative to large groups is the focus of Section 5. We introduce organizational persuasive technology as a method for impacting massive numbers of people very quickly, while still maintaining a personal touch.

In Section 6 we bring everything together and provide encouragement to help your develop and sustain your consistently high-performing organization.

You might notice that this is a relatively short book. As our title suggests, we are all about achieving extraordinary performance at great speed. So is this book. Don't be fooled. It provides you with everything you need to create a high- performing organization.

Now picture yourself at your most serene and successful. Sense how great you feel when you know you have achieved extraordinary organizational and personal success in ways that have helped you personally and advanced your organization. Feels pretty good doesn't it? That's what our process for achieving high performance, and this book, are all about.

Section 1

The Science of High Performance

1

A Proven Methodology

George was the vice president of learning and development for a very large discount retail chain. He had been responsible for the people component of many new initiatives. He learned about this process. but was skeptical. He asked us for a reference from someone who had used the process. We sent him to Karen, the senior training manager of a women's apparel company that targeted a similar market.

George called Karen and they spent two hours discussing how setting the bar worked, how employees were motivated, how the persuasive technology worked – everything! Karen told George that the process worked better than we had described.

Yet George told us he still didn't believe it was possible. Go figure!

The Need for Credibility

The claims we are making in this book are so much better than anyone is used to, and the approach we describe is so different from the conventional wisdom, that almost everyone is skeptical at first. Heather and Kevin did considerable testing before they became believers. We hope we will spare you some of their skepticism by providing you with some context.

Let's Start at the Beginning

The methodology began with a specific business problem at a large high-tech manufacturer in late 1996. We had been working with people there on a particular chip-design project that was struggling. They asked us to help them understand the reasons behind their struggle and give them some guidance.

We discovered that of the 650 people working on this project, six guru chip designers were completely swamped and, to varying degrees, 644 others were wasting time waiting for direction or output from those six. The problem became:

> *How do we get the knowledge out of these six experts and make*
> *it available to more people so they can be more productive?*

In addition, the company told us that we couldn't do this as consultants because they didn't like consultants, but they loved tools. So, this problem would be best solved with some type of technology. That was a challenging set of parameters to say the least.

The Experts' "Secret Sauce"

The first challenge we encountered was that the experts were "unconsciously competent," which meant they couldn't easily tell someone what they knew because they, themselves, were unaware of what they really knew. It took almost 18 months to develop, test and refine a technique that enabled us to consistently and efficiently obtain what we came to call the experts' "secret sauce."

It took almost 18 months to develop, test and refine a technique that enabled us to consistently and efficiently obtain what we came to call the experts' "secret sauce."

This new technique was a true breakthrough. We received national recognition from analysts such as IDC and publications such as KMWorld. We have continued to work with this technique, enhancing and refining it based on our experiences in diverse industries and organizations. Over time this initial technique evolved into the "Wisdom Discovery" process described in Section 2 of this book.

Solving Rest of the Puzzle

Once we knew how to obtain the experts' secret sauce, the next, and bigger, challenge emerged. While people were thrilled with the knowledge we were gathering, no one knew how to use it. This became most acutely apparent when we did a knowledge-gathering program for a major aerospace company. The clients wanted to know how their experts evaluated proposals for sending unmanned spacecraft to the outer planets. This was literally rocket science! All of the scientists were thrilled with the content we obtained. However, when we asked them what they were going to do with it, they told us that they "hadn't really thought about that." Six weeks later the funding was pulled from the "knowledge capture" program primarily because they could not justify the value of the knowledge. That led us to a simple slogan:

What is the value of knowledge that no one uses?

That's right! The answer is zero. Unused knowledge has no value! In hindsight that seems obvious, but at the time this aerospace company, with all its MIT and Cal Tech graduates, hadn't really focused on this issue.

Unused knowledge has no value! In hindsight that seems obvious, but at the time this aerospace company, with all its MIT and Cal Tech graduates, hadn't really focused on this issue.

It was pretty clear that we would soon be broke if we didn't focus on it. We had to find a way to get people to consistently use the expert knowledge.

So we focused in on how people use other people's knowledge, and we came to a surprising conclusion – all of the current market alternatives (Table 1-1) had significant drawbacks, particularly when it came to sustaining and scaling the knowledge.

Training in all its forms (e.g., classroom, videos, e-learning, etc.) was the primary means most organizations used to transfer knowledge. However, this approach was expensive to develop and deliver, and was not very effective at sustaining learning or scaling the learning to large numbers of people.

Category	Pros	Cons
Print Materials	• Low cost of distribution • Can be centrally managed and maintained	• High cost of development • Difficult to adapt • Focuses on "official story" rather than reality • Application of knowledge is responsibility of end user • Limited impact
Training	• Moderate cost of distribution • Classroom pplication of knowledge facilitated by session leader	• Moderate cost of development • Ultimate application of knowledge is responsibility of end user • Moderate impact
Mentoring	• High, immediate impact • Application of knowledge "coached" by mentor • Low cost of development	• High cost of distribution • Limitations on speed of distribution

Table 1-1: Comparison of Learning Approaches

Mentoring was better at transferring knowledge and could drive toward sustained learning, but it was completely unscalable.

Knowledge-management systems were more scalable, but had few means of ensuring high-quality content and tended to give people so much information that it confused them, making the information unusable. They were also expensive and difficult to implement.

Creating Motivated Coachees

Around this same time, we began work with a client in the insurance business. They loved our ability to quickly obtain their experts' knowledge and organize that knowledge so it was easily transferred to others. However, the company's agency managers had little interest in the program. They were too busy running their agencies to be bothered with "more garbage from the home office," as they put it. We needed to find a way to motivate those managers.

Since it was in their own words, they felt as if it were theirs, not something "pushed down from corporate."

As we began working with them we found that it helped to have them read the expert-provided content out loud. We also found that having them put the expert knowledge in their own words and type their own words in place of the experts' words caused a fundamental change in them – they began to take ownership for the initiative. Since it was in their own words, they felt as if it were theirs, not something "pushed down from corporate." This was a huge breakthrough! Much later we would find that by having the managers read, feed back and adapt the language of the experts, we were creating an opportunity for positive visualization and affirmation, both of which are important to motivation. We have continued to refine this process, most recently incorporating the latest research in neuroscience. It has evolved into the process detailed in Section 3 of this book.

The Key to Sustainability

So, we had solved the motivational issue. As we continued to work with customers, though, we found that we could create an initial excitement for the initiatives we worked on, but over time that excitement waned. Sustainability was an issue with other, more traditional approaches as well. To solve this challenge we went back to the drawing board and studied how great coaches create sustainability. Fortunately, we were able to observe coaches in several environments including two technology companies, a fast-food company and a consulting company.

What we found was that great coaches would do two important things to enhance sustainability that poorer coaches typically didn't. Great coaches:

- Asked for clear commitments from the people they coached (i.e., their coachees) and held those coachees accountable.

- Periodically followed up with their coachees to ensure that they understood what was needed and that the coachees were actually practicing the new skills.

We observed that the coaches who did these two fairly simple things substantially increased the sustainability of the initiatives we worked on.

We began to develop techniques for ensuring a sustained response, such as setting up a simple system for guiding individuals to create personal to-do lists that were, in effect, commitments to learning the new capabilities. We also created software that followed up with people by sending them periodic reminders of their commitments. Now, instead of losing that initial enthusiasm, our clients were seeing it sustained and even enhanced over time. Those new findings solved the sustainability issue and formed the basis for the process discussed in Section 4.

Creating the Ability to Scale

What we had developed so far was truly revolutionary. For the first time, companies could quickly and reliably obtain their experts' secret sauce and then organize and present it in a way that would create instant buy-in and motivation. Finally, they now had a way to sustain that initial excitement long enough to see the initiative through to completion. Those were major breakthroughs, but there was one piece of the puzzle left – how could we scale our solution to enough people fast enough to create true high performance across an organization?

If they could influence the attitudes and behaviors of hundreds of thousands of consumers at one time, we reasoned, why couldn't we apply the same approach to organizations?

Our solution was based around a desktop software system at this point, and though the people who used it also loved it, we needed to look at other technologies. It was around this time that we happened on a fairly recent effort through Stanford University called the Stanford Persuasive Technology Lab. This lab was studying software designed to modify the attitudes and behaviors of consumers. This type of software was in widespread use on cell phones, PDAs, and the Web. If they could influence the attitudes and behaviors of hundreds of thousands of consumers at one time, we reasoned, why couldn't we apply the same approach to organizations? This took us back to the drawing board for a complete redesign of our desktop application, transforming it into a Web-based application incorporating persuasive technology concepts.

We began testing the new solution with customers and the results were nothing short of spectacular. Where companies took months or even years to roll out an initiative using traditional learning approaches, we could now get the same (or better) results in just a few weeks. Companies could now go from initial strategy through knowledge discovery and initial roll-out in as little as 10 days, with full implementation across thousands of employees in a few months. This ability to rapidly scale to large numbers of employees is further described in Section 5.

All this may sound easy in hindsight. Not really! The development process we have just described took more than eight years and really reached full maturity only in the last two years with recent advances in the study of neuroscience, particularly the emergence of the field of "self-directed neuroplasticity." It is only with this new science that the final pieces of the puzzle have been put in place, making the methodology described here completely effective, highly predictable and incredibly powerful.

The Proof Is in the Numbers

This methodology has been used in several well-controlled tests that give insight into the impact. The best test was done at a discount auto-parts chain.

The focus of the test was the development and deployment of a new management system intended to both increase sales and give assistant managers more opportunities for growth.

The trial included 48 stores. Sixteen stores used the approach described in this book. Their performance over a three-month period was compared against two control groups – 16 other stores in the same region and 16 stores in another region – that were matched by similar management experience, demographics and sales histories.

The stores were all measured on two key metrics for the industry:

- sales increase against budget

- inventory shrink (a measure of inventory loss from things other than sales)

Once the results were in, the test stores were also evaluated for return on investment.

For every dollar this organization invested in the approach described here, it got $38 dollars back.

The results were a ringing endorsement for the process described here. In 12 weeks, the 16 test stores realized an overall, average 5.25% increase in sales above both comparison groups. In addition, they decreased inventory shrink 30% more than the comparison stores. That resulted in an overall return on investment in the test stores of 38 times their investment. Think of that! For every dollar this organization invested in the approach described here, it got $38 dollars back.

Furthermore, when the 5.25% increase in sales was extrapolated across the entire chain, it translated to more than $200M in additional sales per year, $56M in additional profit per year, and a full 30% increase in earnings per share!

This is just one example of the quantitative results that have been achieved.

What Are People Saying?

In other cases, companies have not had clean, precise impact measures such as those described above. For them, we have had to rely on anecdotes to measure impact. Here are just a few quotes from other organizations about their experience with the methodology described in this book:

- Frank, vice president of manufacturing for a blood-products maker, said: "For the first time ever, thanks to this system, I can go into board meetings and know exactly where we are in an initiative. I love its ability to track progress."

- Kermit, director of marketing for a large technology company, said: "This approach has significantly shortened the time it takes us to define and launch a new product."

- Carl, coaching manager for a financial services company, said: "This system enables us to provide much better follow-up and support for the hundreds of people who attend our seminars."

There are many more, but we are sure you get the idea. The methodology works, and it works in a wide variety of organizations and industries.

THE MODEL FOR ACHIEVING

2

The Model for Achieving
High Performance

We have asked many executives and managers over the years to think about the last critical initiative they attempted to implement. We then asked them how long it took to have it completely implemented to their satisfaction throughout the organization.

Surprisingly, almost 90% of them responded with a resounding "We never finished the implementation!" With many of the remaining 10%, we heard responses like "We're still working on it," "It depends," or "I'm not sure." This is hardly high performance!

So what is it about performance improvement initiatives? It seems as if many are begun with the best of intentions, but few are completed successfully.

This got us wondering whether there was a better way. Recent scientific breakthroughs are providing a better way to achieve high performance.

Why Science?

Achieving high performance is all about motivating people and organizations to change so that they can better align with the vision of the organization and increase their productivity and effectiveness. Such changes require the adoption of new attitudes, behaviors, methods, and even new cultures. Historically, these types of changes have been extremely difficult to achieve. Consequently, it is even more important that the science makes these changes predictable, thereby ensuring that performance improvement actually occurs consistently, systematically and efficiently.

So why should you care whether this approach has a scientific basis? Our strongest proof is the underlying science. It explains how we could achieve high performance so much faster and better than any of the alternatives. It also explains why this entire process is so stable and predictable. If you follow the process defined here you will get the desired results.

If you understand how change occurs then you can create an environment where almost every initiative, program or project can generate predictable, positive results. High performance is achieved not just once in a particular program, but over and over again.

A Scientific and Practical Model of Change

The process discussed in this book is based on the integration of four bodies of recent scientific study – positive deviance, fair process, neuroscience and mass customization.

What does this science mean for high performance? Our extensive experience with this science and its direct application to achieving high performance in organizations has led us to create a simple and extraordinarily effective four-part model of organizational change (Figure 2-1). This model provides a step-by-step solution that you can begin applying immediately. It also enables you to achieve significant change more quickly than previously thought possible. Many of the organizations that we have worked with see an initial change in days, and real performance improvement beginning in just a few weeks!

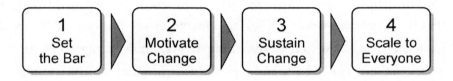

Figure 2-1: A Scientific Change Model

In the following chapter we provide the scientific foundation for each portion of the model, and in the next four sections we provide practical advice for applying the steps to your initiatives, programs and projects.

First, let's provide an overview of the model, introduce each step, and connect each step to the others.

Step 1: Set the Bar for High Performance

The first step in achieving extraordinary performance focuses on development of a clear, comprehensive definition of high performance that translates the organization's overall strategic vision into a practical reality. It is often said:

"If you don't know where you're going,
then any road will do"

That is especially true when it comes to achieving high performance. To be successful, any initiative, program or project must have a clear definition of the desired outcomes that aligns with the definition of high performance.

While this definition can come from many sources (e.g., some consultants will tell you that they know the best way to implement your initiative or how "other companies" have done it), we have found that the very best wisdom comes from inside an organization. It comes from those people who have most consistently and systematically outperformed everyone else in the organization. In other words, it comes directly from your "positive deviants."

Positive deviants are important to achieving high performance because they are often the natural leaders of any performance-improvement initiative. Typically, they already demonstrate many of the attitudes, thought processes and behaviors of the desired outcomes of the change. They have already been successful within your unique environment and culture, so who better to help you define and communicate a model of high performance to the rest of the organization?

Step 2: Motivating High Performance

While it's essential to leverage your positive deviants to create a great initial definition of high performance, that is not sufficient for ultimate success. In order to reach your performance goals, each person participating in a change must be motivated to embrace the model provided by the positive deviants.

In order to reach your performance goals,
each person participating in a change
must be motivated to embrace the
model provided by the positive deviants.

To help with this initial adoption, our model draws on recent advancements in fair process and neuroscience studies of positive visualization and affirmation.

By combining the positive deviant content defined in "Set the Bar" with fair process and the neuroscience of positive visualization, people can be consistently guided to enthusiastically embrace both the larger vision and the more detailed tactics required to achieve it.

Step 3: Sustaining High Performance

Motivating individual change creates initial adopters, but long-term, sustained high performance is possible only when each person practices the new attitudes and behaviors enough to integrate them as a natural part of everyday life. These new attitudes and behaviors must become habitual.

The neuroscience of learning gives excellent guidance for providing people with the repetitive experiences that quickly form desired attitudes and behaviors into habit. That enables the initial change to be sustained over the long term, creating a real and sustainable transformation in the organizations.

Not surprisingly, the deviants' knowledge includes the experiences that resulted in them developing their wisdom. By consciously giving other people experiences similar to those of the positive deviants – first, exposure to the underlying concepts of the positive deviants' knowledge through fair process and positive visualization, then consistent, intense practice of the new attitudes, thinking and behaviors – you can help almost anyone develop the habits required to indefinitely sustain the performance improvement.

Step 4: Scale High Performance to Everyone

Finally, high performance requires that enough individuals change fast enough to reach a critical mass, creating sufficient momentum to cause an organization as a whole to transform. However, a change perceived as too centrally driven is often rejected as overly bureaucratic. To be successful, a change approach must maintain a delicate balance between developing, deploying and maintaining consistent quality standards and processes, and accommodating each person's unique situation. The theory of mass customization and "persuasive technology" provide us with a way to maintain this balance.

The synergies between each step in the model and the overall process create significant performance improvements that are centrally driven, but look and feel as though they are from the grassroots.

3

The Underlying Science (Briefly)

To fully understand the process and how to effectively apply it in your situation, it helps to first understand the underlying science. Of course, you don't need to delve into the science if you don't want to. The process stands on its own and can be applied as described. But it never hurts to know something about the background.

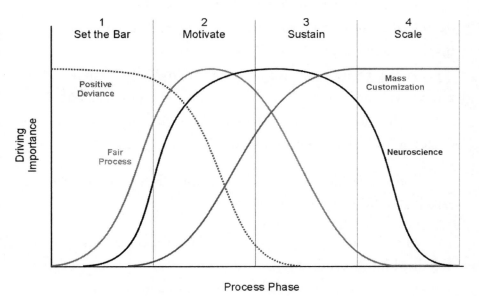

Figure 3-1: Driving Importance of Various Science Areas

The methodology presented here relies most heavily on four underlying areas of science – positive deviance, fair process, neuroscience and mass customization. Each area plays a role throughout the methodology, and each plays a driving role at a specific time (see Figure 3-1).

Set the Bar: The Theory of Positive Deviance

As you may already have figured out, the theory of positive deviance simply states that, within any group, there are a few people who consistently and systematically outperform the others. They "deviate" from the group norm in a "positive" way. These positive deviants have a wisdom that, when leveraged across an organization, can create extraordinary value – especially in achieving high performance.

Research on positive deviance began in the 1980s, and was further developed in the early 1990s with studies of malnutrition in Vietnam by Jerry Sternin and his wife, Monique. At that time, Vietnam was experiencing severe and widespread starvation. Various world organizations had made numerous efforts to solve the problem with little success. The Sternins were able to win a small grant from Save the Children to "fix the problem" in four Vietnamese villages.

Sternin decided to apply an out-of-the-box approach that he called "amplifying positive deviance."

First, he and Monique identified four villages that were particularly hard-hit. Second, they guided people in each of the villages to identify the mothers whose children were not malnourished: that is, to identify the positive deviants within each village. Third, the Sternins got everyone else in the village to do the same things these "positive deviant" mothers were doing with their children, breaking the cycle of malnutrition. Using the Sternins' approach, malnutrition dropped 65% to 85% throughout these villages over a period of just a few months.

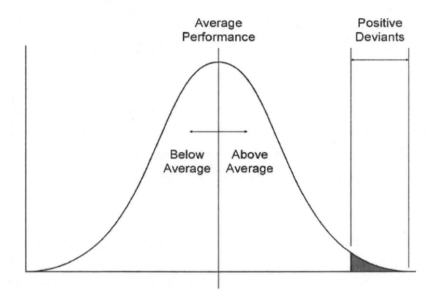

Figure 3-2: Positive Deviance

In the years since the Sternins' work, the concept of positive deviance has been applied to many other situations, including business and organizational development. It turns out that the theory can be applied to all types of organizations. There are positive deviants in virtually every business group, in occupations as diverse as insurance agents, quick-service restaurant managers, school teachers, project managers, and microprocessor designers.

For our purposes, the positive deviants are important to achieving high performance because they hold a large portion of the organization's "tribal wisdom." This expertise gives them the ability to be more efficient than others and to lead others to achieve greater productivity. As such, positive deviants are the foundation for any effort to create a high-performing organization.

As such, positive deviants are the foundation for any effort to create a high-performing organization.

We are confident that you have positive deviants throughout both your own organization and industry, even if you don't think so. In the next section of the book, we will provide a process for identifying positive deviants and discovering their wisdom.

Motivation: Fair Process and Positive Visualization

Two bodies of science provide guidance in how to motivate people to extraordinary performance: the theory of fair process and the neuroscience of visualization. Implemented together, they produce an almost instantaneous, positive response to a performance improvement. They also lay the foundation for sustaining the higher level of performance.

The theory of fair process holds that changes perceived by the participants as being "fair" enhance peoples' willingness to embrace the change and improve performance. Fair process occurs when the following two conditions are perceived to be true:

- The change process is open and transparent

- The change process enhances participants' sense of dignity and honor

Fair process research began with legal research in the 1970s. At a time when people were questioning the legitimacy of many government and legal institutions, researchers began asking questions about the conditions that created a perception of legitimacy (or illegitimacy). They thought that a legal decision would be considered to be legitimate if it created personal benefit and would be rejected if it created personal burden.

However, to their surprise, the researchers found that a legal decision-making process that was open and transparent and that treated people with honor and dignity (i.e. a "fair process") was seen as legitimate even if the decision was against someone's personal interest. Conversely, they found that decisions were not considered legitimate if they were made without transparency or if the process diminished people's sense of self-esteem. In other words, a fair process was more important than the specific results.

Organizational researchers picked up the notion of fair process and applied it to other types of decision-making, including organizational change such as performance improvement initiatives, and found the same result: Organizational changes that met the criteria for fair process were embraced, while those that did not were rejected.

In the methodology discussed here, we are going to guide you to present the positive deviant content using fair process, creating an almost instantaneous acceptance of the change initiative.

People's response to the positive deviant content and fair process is consistent with the recent neuroscience research (the study of human brain function) on positive visualization.

Positive visualization research suggests that when a person internally visualizes a positive outcome to a situation, the positive outcome is more likely to be realized.

Positive visualization research suggests that when a person internally visualizes a positive outcome to a situation, the positive outcome is more likely to be realized.

This research further suggests that when people see themselves as having the same positive capabilities as the positive deviants, neurotransmitters that create a sense of well-being are released, which results in a heightened ability to learn new attitudes, thinking and behaviors. The technical term for this positive visualization is "self-directed neuroplasticity."

"Self-directed neuroplasticity" is a relatively new concept. Until just a few years ago it was thought that our brains did not change much after the age of 18, when they are fully mature. However, research that was initially focused on obsessive compulsive disorder (OCD) and later on stroke victims has shown that each person's brain is much more flexible or "plastic" than previously thought.

For example, even as a person with OCD is involved in an obsessive act, such as repetitively washing his or her hands, a portion of the brain knows that this behavior is abnormal, but he or she cannot stop it. The portion of the brain that suppresses inappropriate behaviors does not work properly. But researchers Jeff Schwartz and Sharon Begley demonstrated that it was possible to use the correctly functioning portion of a person's brain to identify the beginning of an OCD episode and substitute a different, positive image for the obsessive behavior. Practiced enough, this substitution becomes automatic and the OCD is minimized both on MRI scans and in the patient's behavior. Thus, people can literally think themselves out of a negative situation.

Not surprisingly, people can also think themselves into a positive situation. Researchers compared two groups of equally-skilled basketball players shooting foul shots. One group visualized an effective shot while the other physically practiced the shot. In game situations, the visualizing group outperformed the practicing group. By intensely thinking and acting like the positive deviants, people can literally think themselves into the same capabilities as the positive deviants.

By intensely thinking and acting like the positive deviants, people can literally think themselves into the same capabilities as the positive deviants.

For our purposes, we will use the positive deviant content and fair process to guide people to visualize themselves as being as effective performers as the positive deviants. This will cause both a feeling of well-being toward the change initiative and a heightened ability to learn the new capabilities.

Sustaining: Neuroscience of Learning

While the positive response to the motivation step above is a great start, it does not produce a long-term change. Additional science is needed to achieve sustained high performance.

A second area of neuroscience research, the general study of "neuroplasticity," helps us understand how people convert learned behaviors to habits. This research has found that human brains transfer knowledge from short- to long-term memory mainly through repetition. This provides us with important guidance on how to create a sustained impact.

More specifically, neuroscientists have demonstrated that all learning, from infants learning to speak to adults learning new skills, involves changes to the neural pathways. The underlying principle of these changes is: "Neurons that fire together, wire together."

Neurons (think of them almost as tiny spark plugs in the brain) fire whenever there is brain activity. The research has shown that when people learn something, neurons migrate into pathways, packing themselves closer together. The more the learning is practiced, the tighter the packing and the faster the human thought processes.

For example, researchers compared the brain activity of highly trained U.S. Special Forces soldiers with that of regular soldiers in simulated combat. They expected the brain activity levels of the Special Forces to be higher because they could process more information. Conversely, they expected regular soldiers' brain activity to be lower because they would be overwhelmed.

The results were exactly the opposite. Special Forces brain activity was very low while the regular soldiers soared. The researchers determined that, because of the intense training of Special Forces, they were accessing well-established neural pathways around a set of well-learned principles. In contrast, the regular soldiers had to think through all aspects of the situation, making them slower and more prone to significant mistakes. The intense practice by the Special Forces personnel created streamlined neural pathways and significantly better performance.

Now, let's tie the first three areas together. We are going to show you how to take the positive deviant wisdom, present it to people through fair process and positive visualization, creating almost instant engagement, and provide people with sufficient practice to create a habit of high performance.

Scaling: The Theory of Mass Customization

Finally, while this is all very powerful for an individual, how do you make this effective if you have hundreds or thousands of people who need to participate in the initiative? The theory of mass customization guides us in how to obtain the benefits of a mass change while still allowing sufficient personal and local customization to have individual fair process. Mass customization is particularly powerful when supported by a persuasive technology, which we will discuss later.

Mass customization was an approach to manufacturing developed by a team at IBM in the 1990s. This team was led by B. Joseph Pine II. It is a system for balancing the need to have centralized economies of scale, quality standards and consistency (the "mass" part) with the need to adapt to each individual (the "customization" part). Mass customization enables an organization to capture all of the efficiency of large-scale production while effectively treating each person uniquely.

For the process in this book, the concept of mass customization enables the rapid and widespread leveraging of positive deviant wisdom, fair process, positive visualization, and habituation while still enabling each person to customize that content to fit his or her specific situation. Each person feels that he or she is being uniquely treated, but the performance improvement is mass-produced.

Each person feels that he or she is being uniquely treated, but the performance improvement is mass-produced.

The theory of mass customization alone, though, is not sufficient to enable scaling. After all, many people must experience the motivational and sustaining portion of the model in order to create organizational high performance. This requires a technology specifically designed to support both the earlier portions of the model and mass customization. This technology is known as "persuasive technology."

Recent advances in the field of persuasive technology have made real-time mass customization possible. Deriving both from a seminal text in the field, Persuasive Technology, and the founding of Stanford University's Persuasive Technology Lab, persuasive technologies are designed to influence what people think and do. They provide a series of on-screen prompts and flows that create different types of engagement.

In some instances, they are designed to drive an actual sale. In others, persuasive technologies are designed to create long-term engagement with an information source. In the case of organizational changes, persuasive technologies are designed to create immediate engagement around an initiative (i.e. the motivational process) and sustain the engagement (the sustaining part) with schedule planning, notifications and tracking, and to do this for large numbers of people at once. Because of the importance of persuasive technologies, we will devote a later chapter to their use with high performance.

The Result

By combining recent advances in four distinct areas of research (positive deviance, fair process, neuroscience, and mass customization)* any initiative, program or project can be effectively implemented. This new science takes the organization's strategic vision and, in just a few weeks, converts it into an energized, grassroots movement for profound change – change that leads to that high performance.

*Appendix A provides a list of further readings in each of these areas.

Section 2

Setting the Bar
for High Performance

4

Positive Deviants' Secret Sauce

Greg is a positive deviant forecaster at a large high-tech manufacturer. While others struggle to accurately forecast customer sales, Greg is able to generate more accurate forecasts with less effort than any of his peers.

This is due in part to Greg' framing of his forecasts in much broader terms than others. While many of his peers see forecasting as simply entering a number into a statistical forecasting tool, he sees forecasting, in his own words, as "the strategic connection between the company and its customers."

By framing it that way, Greg focuses on learning more about each customer, each division, and many other factors that he systematically integrates into a repeatable weekly judgment about the correct forecast for each customer. Greg regularly demonstrates all the patterns of positive deviance including his passion, efficient actions, excellent risk management, and effective utilization of resources.

When we used the term "positive deviant" with his colleagues and managers to describe Greg, we often got a strange look that says: "What are you talking about?"

Everyone is familiar with deviants. But positive deviants?

Then the idea registers. If you can have deviants that are bad, in other words, "negative deviants," then why can't you have positive deviants, too? Why can't you have people like Greg who are extraordinarily successful?

Positive Deviants' Driving Focus

What makes positive deviants so important for achieving high performance? It is something we call the positive deviant "secret sauce." This secret sauce is their true, underlying tacit wisdom. It consists of their mental models, subtle rules of thumb, early problem-detection mechanisms, attention-allocation processes, and actual work efforts that enable them to consistently outperform others. In addition, it is a deep, passionate commitment to the success of the process that causes the positive deviants to apply their specialized wisdom more intensely and profoundly than nonexperts. Positive deviants are the embodiment of high performance.

The Organization of Positive Deviant Wisdom

More specifically, we have found that the attitudes, cognitive processes and behavioral patterns of positive deviants are always organized around four distinct focus areas (Figure 4-1). We say "always" because our experience shows that positive deviant wisdom is organized this same way independent of the industry, subject matter or specific expertise. These areas play an important role in driving change, so let's take a closer look at each one.

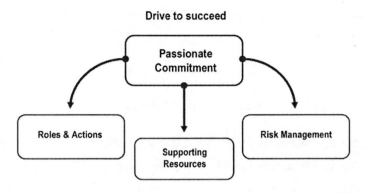

Figure 4-1 – Structure of Positive Deviant Wisdom

Passionate Commitment

First, positive deviants love what they do. Their excitement and commitment is driven by a passionate, if usually unarticulated, desire to achieve a higher social or moral purpose. For example, positive deviant customer service agents in a large call center saw themselves as "the primary link between a real customer need and a great response to that need." Other, less successful customer service agents saw themselves as "placing a product order." The positive deviants took a very mundane task and, mostly unconsciously, converted it into the accomplishment of a greater social good, while the others had a narrower, more tactical and less energizing perspective.

Later we will see how the positive deviant's passion for achieving an internal social or moral purpose aligns with the overall vision for the organization and can be guided into clear, tactical and engaging language. Once the positive deviant social purpose is articulated, it will be used to create a surge of excitement and engagement around your vision, speeding its adoption and helping ensure the ultimate success of your initiative, program or project.

Roles and Actions

Second, positive deviants are extremely effective and efficient at performing key business functions because they are highly organized. In fact, they are quite a bit more organized and efficient than others in the same situations. Specifically, positive deviants achieve their efficiencies by first organizing their work into a sequence of "big steps," which are major phases that systematically build toward achieving an objective. Furthermore, they define each big step with:

- A set of underlying principles that are the primary concepts required to understand the meaning of the big step

- Specific tasks that simultaneously teach the meaning of the big-step principles and guide them to perform the work actually required to achieve the big step

As such, positive deviants' organizational skills naturally help them define the most critical aspects of the initiative, program or project – specifically, the actions required to achieve it.

Risk Management

The third element of the positive deviants' wisdom is their ability to almost instantaneously identify risks. Even more important, they manage them just about as quickly. This enables them to systematically reduce many barriers to their success. (In his book Blink, Malcolm Gladwell describes similar capabilities.) Consequently, the likelihood of a risk significantly delaying or stopping a positive deviant's progress toward his or her goal is sharply reduced.

Supporting Resources

Finally, positive deviants are prolific, though very focused, users of other resources. They can quickly identify the specific resources (manuals, training, other people, etc.) that are the most effective at supporting them.

For example, positive deviants in a manufacturing company identified the one module out of a three-week course that was the foundation for learning a new set of skills in support of a significant organizational change. The rest of the three-week course was irrelevant to the change, but this one module was crucial. As a result, once the organization was made aware of the positive deviants' approach, it refocused the training to teach people the material in this single module rather than the entire course.

The Result

The organization of positive deviant wisdom into these four categories provides the bridge between the strategic vision of high performance and its practical implementation. The positive deviants' commitment to the social or moral good usually aligns well with and supports the strategic initiative, translating the overall vision into a practical reality. Similarly, their ability to synthesize various elements of a situation into practical solutions provides the "how to" for any initiative. Finally, their commitment to achieving the greater objective provides the organization with the fortitude to succeed even where there are many barriers.

5

Finding Your Positive Deviants

We were working with the vice president of human resources in a large manufacturing company to improve the company's widely despised performance-evaluation system for managers. This system was the result of many individual "improvements" over the years, and had become a hodgepodge of disparate criteria, evaluation, and processes. His goal was to design a wholly new evaluation system that was efficient, effective, and avoided the perceived inequities of the current system.

We started by asking him to identify the managers who were best at performance evaluation. Since there were literally thousands of managers, his first response was, naturally:

"I can't possibly do that. How can I know who the best ones are? There are just too many good managers to choose from!"

You might think most people would be overwhelmed by this question, so his initial answer may not be surprising. How could anyone be expected to select, off the top of his head, those managers who were the best at performance evaluations? Certainly, some type of survey or other company-wide analysis would be required first, wouldn't it?

Luckily, the answer is "no." When the theory of positive deviance is applied, there is no need to engage in lengthy and expensive company-wide analyses.

Instead, we asked him to simply close his eyes and visualize his managers. Then, with his eyes still closed, we asked him a simple question:

"Who, for performance evaluations, are your 'go-to' people? In other words, when it comes to performance evaluations, whom do you most respect?"

He thought for no more than a few seconds, then his eyes snapped open and he quickly named 10 managers that he most trusted with performance evaluations. Quite simply, those were his positive deviants.

Surprise! For any given function or area of expertise, almost everyone already knows who the positive deviants are. We have found that people already have an exceptionally rich, highly consistent, comprehensive mental map of the varied expertise in their immediate organization.

We have found that people already have an exceptionally rich, highly consistent, comprehensive mental map of the varied expertise in their immediate organization.

These are their "go-to" people – those few individuals who are consulted when there is a really difficult challenge.

Consequently, instead of having to purchase and develop expensive, ineffective profiling systems, all you have to do is ask your management team three simple questions:

1. Who are the people you most respect for their ability to perform some or all of the functions associated with an initiative, program or project?

2. Are those the people you would go to if you needed to solve a critical problem or identify leadership for a new initiative, program or project dealing with this function or area of expertise?

3. If those people told you how to do something would you (a) believe them and (b) do whatever they said to do, without question?

The people identified by the first question and then qualified by the second and third questions are the true positive deviants. They are the people who are most respected by those actually doing the work. They are the "go-to" people in the organization.

Approached this way, we have found that there is a high degree of consensus on just who the positive deviants are in any given organization. When we asked regional vice presidents at a national insurance company for a list of positive deviant agents, they all named the same people. As we asked others in the same organization, they all listed virtually the same set of people, with only a few exceptions. We have found this to be typical of all organizations that we've worked with.

To an amazing degree, most people in an organization who work in a particular function will identify the same list of people as the most respected in a given function. We even ran a statistical test to determine whether a more formalized statistical process would produce results that were significantly different from those produced by this fast mental process. To our surprise (and great joy), the results were nearly identical! All organizations we tested knew intuitively who their positive deviants were.

Notice that we have not asked which individuals have the best metrics, the most experience, or who are the most liked – all of which are commonly used as criteria to identify so called "experts."

Respect Is Key

Notice that we have not asked which individuals have the best metrics, the most experience, or who are the most liked – all of which are commonly used as criteria to identify so called "experts." Instead, we consistently focus on respect. It is possible to drive metrics in ways that do not create respect, particularly if the metrics are short-term. It is also possible that, because someone is highly respected, he or she receives assignments that make it, at least initially, extremely difficult to produce good metrics. For example, true positive deviants are often asked to head groups that are in trouble or improve relations with particularly difficult customers or divisions. This makes metrics a poor indicator of "real" positive deviance.

Similarly, we have not asked people to focus on experience, because experience does not always equal effectiveness. A positive deviant will always be experienced, but experience alone does not create positive deviance. Positive deviants are respected for how they use their experience, which is quite different from just being experienced.

Finally, we have not focused on "nice" or friendly individuals. While positive deviants are almost always friendly and supportive, they are more focused on achieving the social objective than on creating friends. Respect is not a popularity contest, but a more profound capability to achieve success, even in trying conditions.

But I Don't Have Any Positive Deviants

There are some situations in which organizations may think they have no positive deviants:

- When no one person is a positive deviant in all aspects of the desired performance area

- When something is so new that there is no existing knowledge base within the organization, and therefore, presumably, no experts

- When historical performance has been so poor that no one is respected as an expert

We contend that in all but very extreme cases, there are nevertheless positive deviants within the organization. You can still leverage their knowledge, but finding them is a just a bit more challenging.

It is actually rare for any one person to be a positive deviant in all areas related to a performance improvement. Instead, a person must be highly respected in at least one area directly related to the initiative to be classified as a positive deviant. With initiatives, programs or projects that are large or complex, it is usually necessary to assemble a team of positive deviants, each with a different area of expertise.

With initiatives, programs or projects
that are large or complex, it is
usually necessary to assemble a
team of positive deviants, each with
a different area of expertise.

This is particularly true if you are defining something completely new where many people have partial knowledge. When these individual positive deviants are combined, they can produce something more significant.

Extending this discussion, when something necessary to achieving your performance goals is completely new, you want to leverage your positive deviants as much as possible for several reasons:

- The positive deviants typically think about future directions of the organization and therefore often have some great ideas about how to proceed.

- The positive deviants typically are the experts in how to bring the new initiative into the organization, and you need them because it is extremely rare to be able to create an organization from a blank slate.

- The positive deviants will still be your primary change leaders.

The key to finding them is to add a "future-thinking" element to your notion of respect. You want the people you highly respect both for their current capabilities, at least in a few related areas, and for their willingness and ability to think about the future. Most of the time, the list you make will be identical to the regular list of positive deviants, but sometimes people will be eliminated because they aren't flexible enough. Likewise, others will be added because they are constantly pushing for innovation. In any event, even when doing something new, your positive deviants are the fastest and best way to define a desired end-state.

If you don't think you have positive deviants because of a poor history of performance, we have found that there are always positive deviants, but they tend to be hidden. We have never found an organization that didn't have them. There are always some people who systematically and consistently outperform others and display all of the characteristics of positive deviance, even in poor situations. If you can't think of them right away, it usually means you need to find someone who is closer to the work required for the initiative. If you then ask them the three questions, the positive deviants will emerge.

Finally, we have one cautionary note. Not everyone is a positive deviant, no matter how much he or she might want to be or how much you might want him or her to be. We have found that there are always positive deviants in every functional area, but there are never many of them. When identifying positive deviants for your initiative, program or project, you must resist the desire to "be fair." Selecting positive deviants is not about fairness. It is about finding the true experts for the task at hand.

Selecting positive deviants is not about fairness. It is about finding the true experts for the task at hand.

The Result

Widespread awareness of these "real" experts has two significant implications for achieving the ultimate goal of organizational greatness, as well as the high performance that comes with it. First, because there is such a high level of agreement on whom the positive deviants are, their participation in any related initiative, program or project creates instant credibility. That is true even if the initiative, program or project is completely new to the organization or groundbreaking in nature. Just because the positive deviants are participating, many others will embrace the effort. Second, the content they produce is likely to be significantly more practical and meaningful, and therefore will be seen as more valuable by everyone involved. This quality is critical for the acceptance of any change in the status quo, as we will see later.

6

Discovering Positive Deviant Wisdom

We were at a knowledge management conference several years ago and we heard some very consistent themes.

Professionals with expertise often said: "If I tell someone else everything I know, why would the company continue to pay me?" In many environments, knowledge is seen as power. Losing that power advantage by sharing knowledge is a common fear.

In contrast, we kept hearing from managers that, because of the above reasoning: "We will never get our people to share their knowledge." Their frustration was readily apparent.

Not surprisingly, more than half of the sessions at this conference were about how to get highly skilled professionals to share their knowledge. Most of the ideas had to do with paying for the sharing. But many managers said that they had tried financial incentives without success. They were stumped for a solution.

Engaging the Positive Deviants

For many people and organizations, engaging their positive deviants is a legitimate concern. After all, most people view knowledge as power. The more you know, the more valuable you are and, therefore, the less likely you are to cooperate with others. At least that's what conventional wisdom says.

So how do you get positive deviants to willingly share their wisdom? The key is to reframe the issue. Rather than focusing on giving something up, reframe it to focus on what the positive deviants will gain. This can be accomplished by asking the positive deviants a simple question:

"Would you be interested in spending some time with the few people who are your peers, talking about and planning for 'greatness' in your area of expertise?"

Most true positive deviants jump at this opportunity! They typically voice their excitement by asking a follow-up question: "Who are my peers?" This is a very telling response. It means that they are interested – they want to know with whom they will have the opportunity to converse. In addition, most of the time they also start to talk about what "greatness" means for their area. At this point, you have to take a step back and realize that they have likely never been asked this question before, and it intrigues them.

As soon as they ask this question and begin to discuss "greatness," you know they are hooked! They have already begun to think about how to organize the session and what its goals should be. It is as though this is so interesting to them that they just have to start working on the idea immediately.

Consequently, positive deviants are almost always willing to allocate time and attention to a more complete discussion of greatness – especially with others whom they consider their peers. It's not about what they are giving up; it's really about what they can learn from other experts in their field.

However, there is one caveat. Positive deviants will actively participate in defining an initiative only as long as they see their participation as consistent with their higher purpose and professionalism.

Positive deviants will actively participate in defining an initiative only as long as they see their participation as consistent with their higher purpose and professionalism.

They quickly become frustrated and reject any process that they feel is wasting their time. This makes it extremely important to engage them in a wisdom-sharing process that is efficient and results-oriented.

Discovering Positive Deviant Wisdom

Even though the positive deviants are now excited about sharing their expertise, there is still work to be done. We have found that positive deviants tend to be unconsciously competent, meaning they don't know what they know. Have you ever been talking to someone you consider to be a positive deviant and you have to ask the person to slow down, go back and clarify something he or she said? This is typical. Positive deviants are so comfortable with their knowledge, they often enter a "zone" where they speak in acronyms and conflate, or even skip, steps.

So how can you "discover" something that they don't even know they know?

After working with literally hundreds of positive deviants over the years, we have found one approach works far better than any other – something we call a "Wisdom Discovery" session. Wisdom Discovery sessions ideally bring six to eight positive deviants together for two or three days in a structured (and usually professionally facilitated) environment where they share their wisdom. This size is optimal because it is big enough to allow for synergy and a substantial cross section of perspectives, but small enough to be manageable. Getting a selected group of positive deviants in the same room at the same time brings out an energy and focus that just *cannot be duplicated* any other way.

Here is how a Wisdom Discovery session typically works. The facilitator plays the role of an "ideal employee" who is just joining the initiative, program or project team. Playing the role of a person new to the team or organization gives the facilitator the latitude to ask probing, and sometimes naïve, questions. It also gives the positive deviants the opportunity to "mentor" someone on what they believe is the "right way."

We say that the facilitator is the "ideal" new person because he positions himself as being intelligent, competent and motivated – very much like an employee who is just joining a team and really wants to learn from an expert how to be successful. Unfortunately, this new person just doesn't know how to do it the "right way" and needs the experts to help coach him through the process correctly. We have found that positive deviants just can't resist the opportunity to coach a motivated, eager person to do something the right way. It seems to be in their DNA.

To get the positive deviants to reflect on their own wisdom and to entice them to share it, the facilitator starts by asking them a set of structured questions designed to elicit a thoughtful response. Getting the positive deviants to reflect in this way is important. Remember that most positive deviants are what we call "unconsciously competent." If the facilitator were to just ask them some version of "tell me how to do it," they wouldn't get very far.

Instead, this structured approach helps the positive deviants verbalize their underlying wisdom. These questions are typical of those asked when a naïve person joins an initiative, program or project. Among other things, they include:

- What is the objective of this effort?

- Why are we doing this now? How does it impact the company and its customers?

- What does it do for the company and its customers?

- How is the work organized to best achieve the objective?

- What are the key principles required to achieve this initiative?

- What is the best way to initiate and sustain the initiative?

- What are the key roles that will be required and what are these roles responsible for?

- What stands in the way, challenging the successful completion of this initiative?

These questions are virtually universal to all initiatives, programs and projects. More important, when they are asked of positive deviants, they evoke a specialized kind of story that we call the "naïve person story." This is an energetic, passionate and highly transferable story about how they achieved extraordinary performance.

In response to these questions, the positive deviants almost always start with what we call an "official story." Official stories mimic what the organization might write in a brochure or press release. They are "sanitized" versions that are essentially true, but stated in bureaucratic language that lacks vision, energy and passion. We have found these official stories to be almost universally nontransferable to others. When others read or otherwise hear the official story, they lack engagement and quickly forget about it.

In contrast, by constantly asking, "What is the right thing to do?" after the inevitable discussion that follows each of the above questions, the facilitator causes participants to question themselves and quickly switch from the official story to the "real story." Real stories use more colloquial terms, have a less formal syntax, and are bursting with energy, vision and the positive deviants' passion. Focusing on the real story of how to do something the right way drives the positive deviants to a deeper interpretation of their expertise and a better understanding of how they actually use their expertise in support of the high performance.

> ## Real stories use more colloquial terms, have a less formal syntax, and are bursting with energy, vision and the positive deviants' passion.

The switch from official story to real story usually occurs naturally within the first few minutes and without the participants' even noticing.

Once the positive deviants are discussing the real story, what they really think and do becomes the norm for the session, unleashing a wealth of previously "hidden" and valuable wisdom.

In addition, the energy, realism and detail of the positive deviants' real story establish the foundation for motivating participation. The quality of the real language conveys an immediate impression of expertise and confidence, which is very engaging for others.

Wisdom Discovery sessions can be quite intense, which is why we recommend a professional facilitator. We have conducted discovery sessions that were so intense we couldn't get the positive deviants to stop talking, even when we took a break, turned out the lights, and left the room. They just continued to talk with each other in the dark.

> True positive deviants absolutely love to share their knowledge with others.

True positive deviants absolutely love to share their knowledge with others. Even though conventional wisdom says that it is difficult to get people to participate in developing an initiative, we have found it quite easy when using a structured discovery session.

Wisdom Discovery for a New Initiative

Can you or should you use Wisdom Discovery if your initiative is completely new? The answer is an emphatic "yes." There is a version of Wisdom Discovery called "Stretch Wisdom Discovery"™ that is specifically designed for situations of considerable newness and uncertainty.

Stretch Wisdom Discovery sessions are different from regular Wisdom Discovery sessions in the following ways:

- While you continue to use the positive deviants because they are the best people, you add a "futurist," whose role it is to frequently remind people that they need to create a new future and not just rehash the current processes.

- The facilitator plays a more active role, constantly prodding the positive deviants to think about the future state.

- The session takes a day longer, primarily because the team is generating wholly new content.

Stretch Discovery sessions have significant effectiveness in accelerating organizational improvement. As one manager said, referring to a Stretch Discovery, "We accomplished in three days what would otherwise have taken us six months. The Stretch Discovery process tremendously condensed the development of our program strategy."

The First-Person Form

The results of Wisdom Discovery sessions are incredibly useful, but one further step is needed both to make this content engaging for others and to optimize it for implementation. *It must be converted to the first-person form.*

Usually, coming out of a Discovery Session, the positive deviant wisdom is expressed in third-person language, using terms such as "their," "them" and "your," and being phrased for more generic application. For example, the positive deviants phrased a key principle from a recent session as:

"Great leaders inspire passion in their people."

The above principle isn't bad, and it does embrace a concept that is pretty important. However, if this same principle is converted to the first person using terms such as "I" and "my," it becomes much more compelling to others. When others read it, they will tend to visualize it as if were their own. Using the first person, the above principle becomes:

"I am a great leader because I inspire passion in my people."

You can easily see how the first-person form is more engaging. It also makes it possible to use positive visualization when transferring this principle to others. We will further explore the power of positive visualization in a later chapter.

The Result

The Wisdom Discovery process generates several outcomes, including:

- A significantly improved understanding of the underlying expert process(es)

- A clear, passionate statement of purpose and benefit

- Documentation of the key processes and knowledge required for the initiative

When these outcomes are expressed in the first person, engagement and ultimate transference to others is enhanced significantly.

Section 3

Motivating for High Performance

7

The Importance of Motivation

Forty insurance agents were sitting around the table, arms crossed and frowning in hostility. Jeff, the regional vice president, was talking about yet another program from headquarters. There had been so many poorly developed and deployed programs from headquarters that the agents' immediate response was: "More garbage from the ivory tower."

However, when Jeff told them that Larry and Phil, highly respected positive deviant agents, had created the content, the atmosphere in the room changed instantly. Everyone leaned forward and dropped their arms.

One of them said: "Wow, I didn't know Larry was involved. That's great!"

Someone else said with a tone of disbelief: "Is it really from Larry and Phil? I wondered what they were working on."

Almost as one, the 40 agents then said: "So what did they say?"

Because of their respect for the positive deviants involved, all 40 agents had, at least initially, become extremely motivated. Jeff looked like a hero.

Personal Engagement

How do you create high performance in an organization? We contend that the only way to do it is one person at a time.

High performance requires that each individual actively, consciously and positively embrace your initiatives, programs and projects. So, if you want to achieve your vision, you need to quickly generate intense personal engagement with the positive deviant content. This personal engagement will create the means to put your vision into widespread use.

As suggested by the story at the beginning of this chapter, the first thing that creates engagement with others is the participation of the positive deviants in developing the high-performance model. The respect positive deviants are given consistently leads to an initial, wide acceptance of the content. People want to know what the positive deviants have to say because they appreciate the realistic nature of their perspective and their consistent success.

> People want to know what the positive deviants have to say because they appreciate the realistic nature of their perspective and their consistent success.

In addition, as discussed previously, two areas of recent scientific research – fair process and the neuroscience of positive visualization – provide excellent guidance for creating intense personal engagement. This science shows how to create a deeper, more impactful motivation.

Fair Process

As you may recall, the theory of fair process suggests that engaging people about an initiative, program or project in a way that enhances their sense of personal dignity and honor increases the likelihood that they will embrace the changes necessary to implement it successfully. So, what does this mean in relation to the second step of the model?

In order to feel honored, people must perceive that they are being given an opportunity to have significant influence over an initiative, typically by participating in the development and implementation of the processes required to achieve high performance. When people perceive that they helped create something meaningful, they are much more likely to feel that they have been treated with fair process and, therefore, they are more likely to embrace the initiative.

> When people perceive that they helped create something meaningful, they are much more likely to feel that they have been treated with fair process and, therefore, they are more likely to embrace the initiative.

As it relates to the change process we're discussing here, fair process occurs when people interact with the positive deviant wisdom in a way that gives them the opportunity to see greater potential in themselves. This occurs most directly and powerfully when a person:

- Reads the positive deviant statement of social purpose out loud

- Discusses it with peers and/or supervisors

- Rewrites the positive deviants' statement into their own words.

This intense interaction with the positive deviant wisdom creates a perception that they can achieve the same level of greatness and respect as the positive deviants.

As their self-perception begins to change to one of achieving greatness in this area, people show a distinct, visible physical change. Participants indicate heightened motivation by:

- Leaning forward

- Focusing their eyes more sharply

- Breathing faster.

They also make statements such as:

*"I never thought of the change this way, but
this is a great way to move ahead."*

This type of enhanced engagement and motivation is often apparent within just minutes of being introduced to the positive deviant content. Most important, this initial excitement easily converts into a longer-term commitment.

Positive Visualization

Why does this simple process of reading out loud, discussing and rewriting the positive deviant wisdom create motivation? Recall that the neuroscience research on positive visualization tells us that when people picture themselves engaged in a specific activity and they can clearly see the positive results of that activity, they are more likely to perform the activity at a much higher level. It suggests that by reading first-person statements of the positive deviants' social or moral goals (those discussed in the previous chapter) out loud, people hear themselves speaking as though they had just thought of the social or moral good themselves. For example, insurance agents might read out loud:

"I am a great insurance agent because I ensure that my team provides our customers with great service and superior financial products that give each family member long-term financial security."

Wording the statement in the first person, as we discussed in the last chapter, is key. The reader must believe that the statement is about him or herself, not someone else.

In addition, because they rewrote this statement in their own words, the process drives a further level of personalization and internalization. Not only have the readers heard themselves saying these words as though the words were their own, but they have also written the words in their own language.

As a result, these agents begin to visualize themselves as having the same values and motivations as the positive deviants. Such positive visualization substitutes the positive deviant imagery for their own and appears to drive a release of neurotransmitters that create a feeling of well-being, lowering resistance to change and accelerating learning of the new ideas.

What This Is Not!

Notice that we have not mentioned financial incentives or other types of compliance strategies, such as checklists, as part of motivation. In our experience, incentives and compliance schemes tend to backfire. While they can drive limited short-term responses, they are counterproductive in the long term because they convey a distrust of people's commitment and capabilities. In essence, they create the impression that people can't be trusted to do the job right and must be forced to comply. When people are engaged in this way, their personal honor and dignity is reduced (i.e. fair process is violated), and they tend to resist the change more intensely.

Similarly, people get concerned that the reliance on neuroscience is a form of "brainwashing," which has obvious negative connotations. This is absolutely not brainwashing! All learning, from infancy through adulthood, is achieved by the restructuring of neural pathways resulting from the assimilation of new images. People will NOT accept or learn the positive deviant perspective if it does not naturally align with their own view of the world. However, if the positive deviant's social or moral good does align with the individual's values, learning accelerates tremendously because it appeals to the greatness that is found in each of us.

The Result

Does this positive imagery really have an impact on peoples' engagement and productivity? The answer is "yes." Recent research shows a very strong correlation. Kim Cameron, in Positive Leadership, provides many studies of how positive images and language consistently produce higher performance than less positive language and images. For example, he shows that personal health is better and productivity is higher when environments are perceived as focusing on the positive more than the negative. Consequently, when participants in an initiative see themselves in the same positive terms as the positive deviants, their performance improves.

8

We All Need a Coach

For the past several years we have asked people at companies that we work with the following question: When you really need to know something (i.e., when there is a strong sense of urgency), do you:

1. Read a book or binder on the subject?

2. Go to training on the subject?

3. Pick up the phone and call someone you trust?

Prior to a few years ago, almost 100% of those we asked chose option 3, pick up the phone and call someone they trust. This has been consistent across companies, industries, and even cultures.

We say "prior to a few years ago" because recently a fourth option has emerged. People under the age of about 25 have often said that they go to Google first (not one of the choices we offered). This has interesting implications on many social levels. What is interesting for our discussion here is that these same people also universally say that, if Google doesn't satisfy them, then they resort to option 3 – call someone they trust.

It seems universal, even in the age of Google, that when we really need to know something, we seek support from another person we trust.

Why Coaching?

Although the motivation processes discussed in the previous chapter are incredibly powerful, they become even more powerful when a coach participates in the discussion of the positive deviant content.

Why is great coaching so important to the success of an initiative, program or project? Almost universally, the response to the question we asked in the introductory story suggests that each of us has a personal "go-to" network consisting of people whom we respect. It also suggests that interaction with these trusted coaches and/or mentors is an extremely natural process that provides us with the information and support we need when we need it most. By integrating the positive deviant knowledge and the process discussed in the previous chapter with effective coaching support, people's willingness and ability to engage in a change, even an extremely uncomfortable change, increases dramatically – and that has far-reaching implications for improving performance.

Figure 8-1: Nature of Great Coaching

How does coaching facilitate motivation? When we studied the communication styles of great coaches, we found that they would commonly say things like:

- "I'm so glad you called."

- "This is a great project, thanks for including me."

- "This project is going to change the world – I want to be part of it."

In addition, their motivation is almost always tied to their desire to make some significant contribution to others, as we discussed earlier. This desire is contagious, exciting others toward the same goal.

Effective Coaching

Now, having a great mentor or coach who is both a highly respected expert and a great communicator would be wonderful for everyone, but this is not usually possible for several reasons. First, the great coaches and mentors have to be both content experts and great communicators (Figure 8-1). As we discussed earlier, most experts are unaware of what they know so they are inherently limited in their ability to be great coaches.

Second, not everyone is a great communicator. Some of the smartest people seem to be challenged in speaking coherently.

Third, having your best people spend significant amounts of time coaching others does not create optimal organizational leverage. In general, organizations want these great people to be inventing new products, processes and services, not spending their time "babysitting" others.

So how can you provide effective coaching support to people when there are so many barriers? This is another place where positive deviants help. We can simplify this challenge by separating the requirement for expertise from the requirement for communication skills. As a result, one person does not have to be great at both, which makes it easier to find and train coaches. By using the expertise of the positive deviants to meet the requirement for expert knowledge, it becomes much easier for the coach to focus on helping people through great communication.

A portion of this process is therefore designed to help make people great communicators or "coaches."

A portion of this process is therefore designed to help make people great communicators or "coaches." Fortunately, the structure of the positive deviant content and the processes outlined previously make it substantially easier to be a great communicator.

Recall that a participant, or coachee, reads the content out loud, discusses it, and rewrites it in his or her own words. As this occurs, a coach has to do only three things to be incredibly effective:

1. Listen carefully to the coachees as they discuss the positive deviant content, asking probing and clarifying questions.

2. Encourage the coachees to internalize and rewrite the positive deviant content.

3. Continuously praise the coachees for their good work.

Listening to the coachees' responses and encouraging them to talk and write honors their thinking, which is part of fair process, thereby creating legitimacy. Also, praise has been shown to trigger neurotransmitters similar to those released during direct positive visualization, and writing down their interpretation causes people to mentally process the content more profoundly. When a coach does these simple things, learning is quicker and more complete.

Notice that this support is not coaching in the sense of psychological counseling or personal development. This type of coaching, which we call "content" coaching, is solely about a limited set of capabilities that a coach uses to directly support the learning and application of the positive deviant content. Content coaching is much easier to learn than more abstract forms of coaching. Ironically, even though it is easier to be a great content coach, content coaching actually produces many of the same benefits of other forms of coaching. As learners are guided to master the positive deviant content, their confidence increases, they report significant personal growth, and they seem to be more fulfilled.

Who are these "optimal" coaches? Using the process discussed in this book, they can be almost anyone who has a natural supporting relationship with the coachee. In corporate environments it is often the direct manager, though it is also sometimes a technical specialist or trainer. In consulting and training companies, which are selling their knowledge, it is often a paid specialist. It can really be anyone who is already providing support.

Resistance to Being a Coach

While it is ideal for everyone to have a coach, there are some challenges. Surprisingly, the coaches tend to resist taking the time to discuss and focus on the new initiative more than the coachees. As an illustration of the problem, we conducted a survey of a large number of managers in a variety of U.S. corporations, asking them the following two questions. The first was:

How critical is it for you to develop your people?

The answer was almost always something like:

It is one of the most important things I/we do.

This is a good start. We then followed up with:

When was the last time you consciously worked on developing your people?

Unfortunately, the answer to this second question was almost always:

I don't remember when we last did any personnel development, but it was a long time ago.

What a disconnect! They say developing their people (which is usually done through coaching) is one of the most important things they do, but they rarely do it.

Similarly, we were working with another food chain and asked the district managers how they would feel if all of their restaurant managers were as good as their positive deviants. We thought they would be thrilled, since a substantial portion of their income came from restaurant sales. They would make a lot of money from improving everyone's performance.

Instead, they were terrified. One of them told us:

"If everyone is as good as my best people, what would I do?"

To this district manager, the idea that everyone could be a high performer meant that there would be many fewer crises, and, in his perception, the chain would not need him, since he saw his job mainly as responding to crises.

Obviously, neither of those responses is a prescription for high performance. In fact, the single biggest barrier to the success of this program is middle management's unwillingness or inability to take the time to systematically develop their people.

Overcoming the Coaches' Resistance

Fortunately, there are some simple ways to overcome the coaches' resistance in most organizations. They are:

- Guide the coach to see the personal and moral value of developing their people.

- Teach them new leadership skills that enable them to see and develop new work opportunities.

- Hold them accountable for the development of high performance in their people.

First, coaches can be guided to see the moral value of developing their people with a series of direct questions that leverage the positive deviant respect and expertise:

- Is the content that came from the positive deviants good enough that everyone would benefit from performing that way? (If the positive deviants have been selected correctly and the Wisdom Discovery has been done correctly, the answer is always "yes.")

- Is the content good enough that you are willing to spend two hours making sure people understand it? After all, what is the value of content that your people don't understand? (Again, they say it is worth two hours.)

- If the content is this useful, don't you want to be sure that people actually use it? (Again, "yes.")

When coaches respond to these very simple, logical questions, they realize that they have a moral obligation to help their people learn and use the positive deviant content. Anything less is unacceptable.

Second, not surprisingly, as part of this discussion, the coaches begin to reflect on their role in achieving high performance. When we train people in coaching, they always initially focus on the above questions for developing their people, then partway through they realize that becoming a good coach is actually about developing their leadership capabilities. As one coach put it:

*"Superficially, this looks like you are helping me improve
my people's performance, but what you are really doing
is teaching me how to be a great leader."*

Bingo! By following the model, middle managers are subtly guided to learn the skills of what some people call "transformational leadership."

Transformational leaders help others understand and align with a greater purpose, define the actions needed to achieve the purpose, and become extraordinarily high performers, making enormous contributions to the organization.

Transformational leaders help others understand and align with a greater purpose, define the actions needed to achieve the purpose, and become extraordinarily high performers, making enormous contributions to the organization. This is, of course, exactly what this model does.

Consequently, many of the coaches come to feel that this entire model is for their personal development and they therefore embrace it.

Third, while these two approaches overcome the bulk of a coaches' resistance in most cases, to be truly successful the organization must also hold people formally accountable for developing their people and achieving high performance. What this means is that management must be ready to confront resistance to change. As one executive put it to his management team:

"We have been working on this program for nearly a year now — testing it, proving its impact and generally making sure we are doing the right thing.

Either you are going to proactively support this
or you are going to find another job!"

How is that for commitment to achieving high performance!

When all three of these approaches are combined, middle managers tend to both align with the initiative and become enthusiastic supporters of the process, making a significant contribution to extraordinary performance.

The Result

When managers or others are really involved in their coaching role and they use our approach to leverage positive deviant content, they invariably say that the discussions they have with their coaches are among the best they have ever had. They also say that this process produces common perspective and deep alignment faster and more completely than they thought possible. Thus, by exercising a little leadership influence, you can drive the coaches into meaningful support of the initiative, making a significant performance improvement much more likely.

Section 4

Sustaining
High Performance

9

The Importance of Practice

In Chapter 1, we described a controlled test of the methodology with an auto parts chain. Recall that:

- *The company was implementing a new and, for that chain, quite different management structure in its stores. This new approach was designed to provide additional focus on retail sales and more opportunities for assistant store managers to develop the skills required to eventually be great store managers.*

- *The test compared the results of 16 stores that used our approach to change with 16 stores in the same region and 16 stores in another region, all 32 of which used the organization's traditional approach to change.*

- *At the end of the 12-week test, the stores using our approach significantly outperformed the control stores.*

When asked how a difference in performance this large was possible, the managers of the test stores said, "We don't know. We haven't done anything differently." We knew this wasn't true. The data showed that they were doing things very differently. We pointed out to them exactly how their attitudes and behaviors had changed from "business as usual," but they continued to say that they had not changed.

In fact, the changes had been so completely internalized that they couldn't see them. They simply didn't remember ever having acted differently. They lived the new structure every day, in every way, and had the results to prove it. These new attitudes and behaviors had become their "new reality."

As it turns out, we should not have been surprised by that reaction. Recent studies found that most people, after they change their behavior, reconstruct their own memories in such a way as to truly believe they always acted in a certain way. This is key to sustaining high performance. If it's done right, members of the organization won't remember ever behaving in the old way.

Sustained high performance occurs
only as a result of long-term deep
impact within the organization,
not just the immediate thrill of
getting everyone excited.

Sustained high performance occurs only as a result of long-term deep impact within the organization, not just the immediate thrill of getting everyone excited. It doesn't do you or your organization any good to have the positive deviants create a great image of success and have everyone motivated, only to find that the initiative, program or project is seen as just another fad.

True success comes when your leadership and fortitude guide the organization until your initiative, program or project brings about changes that are so ingrained they become the norm. This is the point at which everyone in the organization becomes "unconsciously competent" at the new behavior, living it every day.

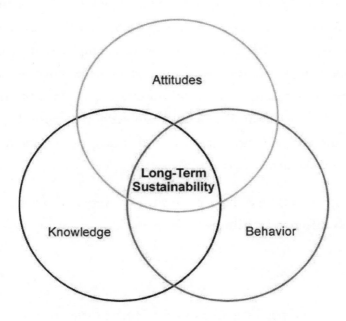

Figure 9-1: Nature of Long-Term Sustainability

The advances in neuroscience previously discussed in Chapter 3 provide guidance on how to make short-term excitement become long-term integration of attitude, knowledge and behavior (Figure 9-1). From neuroscience we have learned that "neurons that fire together wire together." This tells us that long-term learning occurs when neural pathways are exercised enough to form into new structures.

This is similar to the way muscles grow and strengthen as you exercise them. These new neural structures provide the learner with rapid, effective thought processes that are aligned with positive deviant content and therefore support the vision. In fact, with enough exercise, these new pathways become so deeply internalized that people don't even recognize, as we discussed earlier, that they used to think and behave differently. As an example, recall the research on the neural activity of the U.S. Special Forces soldiers cited earlier. The intense training of the Special Forces led to reduced brain activity because the soldiers were extremely efficient at accessing a completely internalized set of underlying principles. Those principles enabled them to handle almost any combat situation "automatically." In contrast, the regular soldiers had a significant increase in brain activity because they were thinking through the entire scenario each time, causing them to be slower and make many more mistakes.

In order to achieve high performance, everyone needs to be as completely effective at their own jobs as the U.S. Special Forces are at theirs.

Practice Makes Performance

How do you sustain extraordinary performance? Practice! Practice! Practice!

The single most important factor in driving neurons to fire together so they will wire together, and produce the type of internalization described in the opening story, is continuous practice. We've said it before, but it is important enough to repeat several times. The new capabilities required for the initiative must be practiced long enough and with sufficient frequency to drive the neural restructuring that is the essence of comprehensively internalizing change.

Not all practice is the same, though. Two elements are required to create a foundation for your team's effective, long-term change:

- Each person must conceptually understand the set of principles underlying the initiative, program or project so each knows what he or she is practicing.

- The principles must be consciously and frequently applied by each person in a variety of situations, consistently and repeatedly, so he or she knows how the principles really work.

The new capabilities required for the initiative must be practiced long enough and with sufficient frequency to drive the neural restructuring that is the essence of comprehensively internalizing change.

Practicing the Right Thing

Why are the principles of a function so important? As our golf instructor always tells us, "Practicing the wrong swing doesn't do a lot of good, even if you practice it a lot!" As is suggested by the Special Forces research, focusing on the underlying principles gives people a broader view of the situation. Once this broad foundation exists, it is much easier to learn and sustain specific tactical responses to individual situations.

This is not as easy as it might sound. The underlying principles involve subtle judgments that each person must learn. In addition, they must be applied in a wide variety of ways and exercised in an equally wide variety of situations.

The primary source of these underlying principles is, of course, your positive deviants. Remember that part of Wisdom Discovery is the definition of the big steps provided by your positive deviants. These organize the overall approach to the initiative, program or project. Furthermore, as part of Wisdom Discovery, your positive deviants also identify and articulate the key principles that define each big step. A good principle expresses not only a key idea, but also why that idea is important. For example, for a recent customer's program on enhancing leadership, a key principle was:

I am aware of and honest about my personal strengths and challenges. My awareness is the foundation of the authenticity needed for people to believe in my leadership.

This principle describes a key attribute of a leader – self-awareness – in the first person along with the reason this attribute is so important. As such, it provides a foundation for activities that will create self-awareness and, ultimately, authenticity.

Recall, too, the process of reading out loud, discussing, and rewriting the statement of the objective provided by the positive deviants. When participants use the same process with each principle, particularly using the first person, they develop a profound understanding of the conceptual meaning.

Each participant creates, within him or herself, the conceptual framework of the principle – what it means and why is it important. This enables them to apply the principles to real situations, adjusting their actions as needed by each unique situation they encounter.

When participants use the same
process with each principle,
particularly using the first person, they
develop a profound understanding
of the conceptual meaning.

Applying the Principles

However, it's not enough to just understand the principles. Everyone working toward higher performance must be given opportunities to apply each principle in a number of different situations. Frequent application of the principles in a variety of real situations is naturally the most powerful method for actually learning them completely. Unfortunately, finding "safe" opportunities for the right type of "practice" can be challenging. Good opportunities for applying the principles must achieve several objectives simultaneously, including:

- They must be an integral part of the current work, so it is perceived as natural and not as an additional work burden.

- They must teach a new consciousness that aligns with the principles and vision for doing the current work, so people begin to become subtly aware of the new perspectives.

- They must give people practice at doing the work the new way, not the old way.

Here is an example of a task that meets these criteria (from a program for how to do great new product planning):

I identify a great new product planner and observe three things
he/she does during a planning meeting that build agreement
on his/her proposal. In my next meeting, I try one of
the observed methods of building agreement.

Notice that the learner is doing something that is part of his or her normal work – attending a planning meeting. Notice, too, that in order to observe how the great planner builds agreement, the learner is driven to think about the processes used to build agreement. Finally, notice that he or she is asked to actually try what has been observed. Just by doing this task, the learner has a multifaceted experience with building agreement. All of those elements contribute to his or her understanding of great new product planning.

As participants do more of these types of tasks, their overall awareness – first of the principles underlying a given big step, and finally of the overall social objective – gradually increase until the new participant is functioning just like the positive deviant.

As may be obvious, this is not classroom "fire-hose training," in which massive amounts of content are dumped on people in a short time. Rather, it is a "slow drip" process, in which each experience gradually and systematically builds on the previous experiences, culminating in deeply learned new attitudes and behaviors.

When approached this way, the change process results in minimal personal and organizational disruption and, at the same time, maximum impact. Most people are not even fully aware that they are thinking and functioning differently – just like the positive deviants.

Barriers to Sustained High Performance

Not surprisingly, while it is relatively easy to get people excited about something for a few minutes, it can be quite difficult to keep them engaged long enough to completely internalize new attitudes, thinking and behaviors. There are several barriers to full internalization:

- Organizations always have significant short-term pressures, and resist allocating time for the practice.

- Organizations have short attention spans, so they expect excellence sooner than it can be achieved.

- People do not like to practice something new.

Can an organization develop high performance if it never allocates time or resources to get better at its work? While it may be possible, it is not likely. Development of any capabilities requires effort, and effort means that something else must stop to make room for work on the improvement.

Development of any capabilities requires effort, and effort means that something else must stop to make room for work on the improvement.

Similarly, can an organization develop high performance instantaneously? Again, it may be possible to have a spontaneous "ah-ha" moment that leads to higher performance, but these moments are normally few and unpredictable. Any significant individual and organizational learning takes time. If your organization lives so much in the moment that it doesn't allocate time for development of its people, but still expects to be excellent, it is deluding itself.

In fact, this is where management commitment to achieving high performance will be most severely tested. You will likely hear many reasons why the change you are requesting can't reasonably be achieved. If you accept those reasons – or, more correctly, those excuses – you will never achieve high performance. If you continue to press for excellence, and use the process described here, you virtually ensure that the organization will achieve it.

The third barrier, though, is a little different. Most people do not like to practice anything, even if everyone intellectually knows that practice is required to create sustained success. Any successful athlete or musician will tell you that he or she practices constantly – but few actually like it. They may not like to practice as much as is needed to be good, but they recognize that intense practice is necessary to achieve excellence. Someone once said that "successful people do what unsuccessful people don't want to do," and practice is one of those things.

This resistance to practicing is particularly apparent approximately six weeks into a change effort. People consistently encounter a significant motivational barrier about that time. This barrier normally shows up as common statements such as: "This is too hard" or "I don't have time to learn this." Resistance to change is common.

Each of those can be a significant barrier to achieving high performance. When all occur together, and the organization does not proactively manage them, performance improvement initiatives can come to a halt.

Much of this resistance to change has a physical basis. Researchers have noted that people typically describe a sensation of physical discomfort that appears to be caused by a tension between learning the new behavior patterns, which are not yet dominant, and letting go of the old patterns, which are still strong (Figure 9-2).

Fortunately, it appears that this feeling of discomfort, and related resistance to change, is actually a false signal from the brain similar to the one that occurs in obsessive compulsive disorder (OCD) patients. Researchers found that coaching OCD patients to ignore the strong signals driving their OCD behavior and substitute positive images, long enough and consistently enough, allowed new brain patterns to form, which significantly improved their OCD.

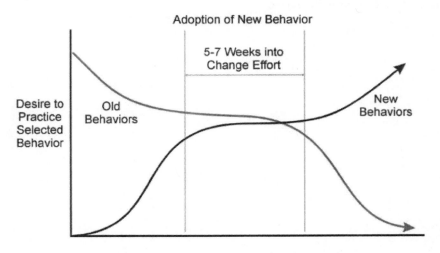

Figure 9-2: Tension Between New and Old Behavior

The same ideas apply to overcoming the resistance to the changes required to achieve high performance. Remember that "neurons that fire together wire together." So, to create new brain pathways consistent with those of the positive deviants and, thus, new thought patterns, it is important for initiative participants to ignore the "false," de-motivating signals and continue to practice the new behaviors for several more weeks. As the saying goes: "No pain, no gain!" In the next chapter we will present some approaches for overcoming these barriers.

The Result

Is creating a sustained change worth the commitment and effort? People frequently tell us that this type of long-term change is incredibly valuable for themselves and their organizations. Imagine that all of your people are like Special Forces personnel, but in support of extraordinary performance. Imagine how skilled and effective everyone is. What would it mean to you to have your own Special Forces team in support of your initiative?

10

Follow-Up Is Everything!

We were working on a long-term engagement a few years ago when we encountered a rather interesting behavior pattern. See if it sounds familiar.

The senior management would introduce a change initiative to the organization. The introduction would be accompanied by lots of fanfare – large, professional presentations, slick procedure documents, and lots of management "cheerleading." But, the funny thing was that nobody in the organization actually did anything differently as a result of management's efforts. They attended the rollout presentations and then just "filed" the documents.

When we asked people why they weren't implementing the changes management wanted, their response was, "It's just the initiative du jour – wait a while and there will be another one."

Other clients have seen this result when trying to implement initiatives. People within the organization treat the initiative as the "fad of the week," sometimes saying that if they "ignore it long enough, then it will go away."

Does the above experience sound all-too familiar? What's really important for creating long-term high performance is not only the introduction, but also the follow-through. An organization's leadership must both expect people to learn and change, and continue to monitor the results of those changes throughout the life of the initiative. More specifically, sustained change requires constant, highly systematic follow-through including:

- Systematic reinforcement of the coachees' learnings

- Regular tracking of progress to ensure that the practice occurs with the frequency required for success, and that support is provided in a timely manner if there are problems

- Explicitly holding coaches and other managers accountable for the progress of their people.

Systematically Reinforcing Learnings

The process of applying the principles to create in-depth learning through repetitive practice, which is already quite powerful, must be further strengthened by systematically recording the lessons learned. It is well-known that reflection on actions causes us to internalize learning.

There are two types of reflection that are easy to do and add considerable value. After the learning task is completed, the learner:

- Writes down what was learned. This can be in the form of a document, presentation, e-mail, etc.

- Presents the key learnings to someone else.

Both of those drive more learning from an action. For example, let's extend the previous task to include those additional modes of reinforcement. It now reads:

> *I identify a great new product planner and observe three things he/
> she does during a planning meeting that build agreement on the
> proposal. In the next meeting, I try one of the observed methods of
> building agreement. I make a slide showing three things I learned
> about building agreement and present the slide to a peer.*

Writing down the lessons extends the consciousness of the learning by forcing people to articulate key ideas (notice that the number is limited so it forces focus). Making presentations to someone else cements the learning because it places still further demands on the natural internalization process.

By the time people have read, discussed and rewritten the principle, practiced it in various ways, and then recorded and presented their learnings, they really know it. When this process is clearly a natural extension of their jobs, it does not feel like a burden, but rather it is perceived as an opportunity to improve. Even though it feels completely ordinary to them, something quite extraordinary is occurring. They are being subtly transformed to a new understanding of and commitment to high performance as defined by the positive deviants.

Tracking Progress

It is often said that "what gets measured, gets done." This is certainly true of any change initiative, program or project. Tracking both individual and organizational progress is critical for several reasons:

- Individual tracking further drives reflection, which drives additional learning.

- Management tracking both sends a message of engagement and enables faster interventions if there are problems, particularly at the six-week barrier.

For individuals, tracking simultaneously reinforces the importance of practicing, drives personal reflection, and makes people feel guilty if they don't perform up to expectations.

Because most people have an aversion to being tracked, we have found that tracking for individuals is most effective when it is modeled after an existing natural behavior, the personal "to-do" list. How many of you keep a "to-do" list? Most people do. How many of you like crossing things off your list? Almost everyone likes this experience. Why is crossing something off a to-do list so rewarding? It appears that people like the sensation of recognizing their own accomplishments, even if no one else even sees the work.

It appears that people like the
sensation of recognizing their
own accomplishments, even if no
one else even sees the work.

So the first reason individual tracking is so powerful is that, most of the time, it makes people feel good.

At the same time, tracking drives further reflection on performance. People who have to record their progress for someone else to see are forced to reflect on the work they did. Typically, people ask themselves reflective questions such as:

- Did I complete the task?

- How did it go?

- What do I have coming up?

The act of recording progress causes people to think about the meaning of progress and, ultimately, the relationship between progress and high performance.

Finally, there is some guilt (in a good way) associated with individual tracking. People know they should be practicing because it is the right thing to do, and tracking keeps reminding them when they are not doing the right thing. If we go back to our "to-do" list idea: How do most people feel about items on the list that never get crossed off? They hate them. Tracking is like being nagged by someone who really cares about you. You know it is for your own good, but you don't really want to hear it. Eventually, though, because you know it is for your own good, you do the right thing. In that sense, for individuals, personal tracking is always in support of their own high performance.

Management tracking is a little different, though. The leader can create a compelling vision, enlist the organization's positive deviants to develop a great road map for success, and motivate the team. But, if the leader doesn't track what's actually getting done, interest and energy quickly wane. An absence of tracking sends a message that management really doesn't care, while close tracking and effective, supportive follow-up sends a message that the performance improvement initiative is critical.

This is particularly important at the six-week barrier we discussed in the previous chapter. At six weeks into a performance-improvement program, individuals, and indirectly organizations, consistently encounter a significant motivational barrier (Figure 10-1). At this point in the process, participants often express substantial resistance to the personal changes required to align with the initiative. Typically, at six weeks, not only do people complain more, but also their progress slows drastically. People stop updating their statuses and often seem to stop working on the initiative all together. Coaches begin to shift their attention from creating the in-depth learning to surviving daily pressures. Recall that this is caused by the tension between the new, emerging neural pathways and the older, established pathways.

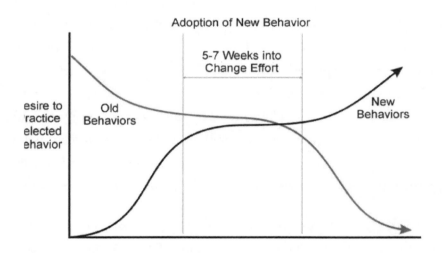

Figure 10-1: Tension Between New and Old Behavior

Management tracking is critically important to both overcoming this six-week barrier and giving the new capabilities the optimum opportunity to dominate. Systematic progress tracking helps management identify the onset of the six-week barrier and take appropriate action, usually just reminding people to keep practicing by sticking with the plan. This additional practice drives the integration of the new patterns sufficiently to remove the conflict between old and new behaviors, and the sensation of discomfort simply disappears.

For most people, like the auto-parts group described in previous chapters, continuous practice drives integration of the new capabilities into daily life. It does this in a way that is so subtle and comprehensive that eventually people often reject the idea that they ever functioned differently. Even when we have crystal-clear data that demonstrate a change in attitude, thought and behaviors patterns, it is quite normal for people to claim they never functioned in the old way.

> Even when we have crystal-clear data that demonstrate a change in attitude, thought and behaviors patterns, it is quite normal for people to claim they never functioned in the old way.

They look at the data and then, with a straight face, say that our data must be wrong! This is when you know you've succeeded!

Accountability Matters

While everything we have done so far makes it much easier for an organization to achieve high performance, it is very difficult to sustain such performance without people being formally held accountable. Tracking is a means of creating accountability because it shows actual performance. As such, tracking-driven accountability occurs in several ways:

- The learner is accountable for working hard to upgrade his or her performance.

- The coach is accountable for supporting the learner and, if needed, providing consequences.

- The management team is accountable for allocating the time and resources needed to execute the program and for continuously staying visibly involved with the initiative.

What does accountability mean? In the extreme, on the positive side, it means being promoted and receiving recognition. On the negative side, it means being terminated. For example, we have seen people who took the process described here seriously very consistently outperform others, and they were appropriately rewarded for their improvement. Conversely, we have seen several situations in which managers and coaches were terminated because they did not support the process in any meaningful way.

There is an obvious structure here (Figure 10-2). The coach holds the individual accountable, the management team holds the coach accountable, and presumably someone holds the management team accountable for its performance.

In that sense, if an individual succeeds or fails, then the coach succeeds or fails. If the coach succeeds or fails, then the management team succeeds or fails. If the management team succeeds or fails, then the organization achieves high performance or struggles, perhaps failing completely. Everyone is connected.

Ultimately, in order to achieve high performance, the organization must be committed enough to the initiative that management is willing to use its authority to both push back when people complain and follow up with them regularly to ensure that they continue working on the tasks.

Here's where commitment gets tested. If the organization isn't committed enough to reward people who work hard and hold less-engaged people accountable, particularly the coaches, then we can say, with almost 100% certainty, that eventually people will find a way to avoid making the necessary changes.

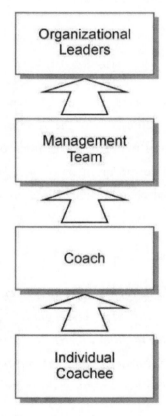

Figure 10-2: Accountability Structure

> By tracking and holding people
> accountable for progress, management
> sends a strong message that it cares
> both about the initiative, program
> or project and about the people.

But, by tracking and holding people accountable for progress, management sends a strong message that it cares — both about the initiative, program or project and about the people.

The Result

As a result of this process, most people, regardless of their personal background, skills or values, learn the new capabilities — attitudes, cognitive and behavioral patterns — required to fully align with and accomplish the initiative, program or project goals. This is the type of sustained, individual change that ultimately creates the leadership moment.

As one recent coachee put it:

"When I first started this project, I thought it was a useless set of tasks that my coach pushed me into. Then, I gradually realized that these tasks were teaching me to think differently. Later, I realized that my new thinking was my new job and, without my ever realizing it, I was doing my new job. I changed completely and I loved it."

At least for one individual, a moment of achieved greatness is now possible.

Section 5

Scaling High Performance to Everyone

11

The Need for Leverage

When you talk with Lee, founder of a financial services company, you instantly feel his passion and wisdom for thinking about family wealth differently. In person, Lee is amazingly powerful.

When you sit with Tom, vice president at a large restaurant chain, you get an immediate feeling of excitement and energy about the possibilities of running a great quick-service restaurant. In person, Tom is incredibly influential.

When you watch David, founder of a very successful group podiatry practice, talk about the future of podiatry, you can feel and see the strength of his vision. In person, David is charismatic and persuasive.

But Lee can't talk personally with all of the thousands of people who attend his seminars. Tom can't possibly sit down with all of his 1,000-plus restaurant managers, 180 area coaches, and 11 regional managers. David can't present to all of the 15,000 podiatrists in the United States. All of them need to have their vision touch hundreds or even thousands of people to be successful. They must somehow extend their personal impact to the masses.

High performance is achieved when large numbers of people collectively operate more effectively. All organizational change is ultimately the cumulative result of many individuals changing together. While it is possible to guide an individual to extraordinary performance through one-on-one contact, personal contact alone is not sufficient to create the large-scale impact required for long-term organizational success.

Of all the process steps we've talked about, scaling is the most abstract. It is also where the differences between our approach and more traditional approaches are most apparent.

Let's illustrate this by telling a little more of Heather's story. When Heather first experienced a Wisdom Discovery, she thought it was incredibly valuable and powerful. We told her that Wisdom Discovery represented less than 10% of the value of this process and that the payoff was really when she could scale the program to hundreds or thousands. But she was dubious.

Then Heather experienced the motivational step in the model, which she thought was extremely exciting and effective. We told her that the motivational portion represented only an additional 15% of the value, and reminded her that the payoff was really when she could scale the program to hundreds or thousands. But she was still dubious.

Next, Heather experienced the sustaining step in the model, which she thought was very profound and important. We told her that the sustaining portion represented only an additional 25% of the value, and again reminded her that the payoff was really when she could scale the program to hundreds or thousands. But she was still dubious.

Finally, she experienced the scaling when, in the space of 10 days, she went from program introduction to a full, global deployment touching hundreds of people literally around the world. At this point, she realized that the high-performance payoff was when everyone improved their performance in alignment with the same vision. As she put it:

> *"Now I get it! Having hundreds of people all motivated to use the positive deviant content and working hard to internalize their learning — everyone around the world working toward the high performance goal — is just an amazing experience."*

It took direct experience with the ability to touch large numbers of people at once, and the sense of empowerment this created, for Heather to understand the value of scaling. Yet, in our view, scaling is the most critical portion of the entire methodology. It makes it possible to leverage reasonable performance improvements for a few people into a truly high-performing organization.

Previous Attempts at Scaling

Some of the doubt that Heather and others feel is likely based on their experiences with the old paradigms. Prior to development of the approach discussed here, scaling just didn't work very well. If you wanted to scale a change initiative to hundreds or even thousands, you basically had just a few choices. You could:

- Hire a large number of trainers and/or consultants to go out into the company and provide hands-on coaching to everyone

- Bring all of your people into a classroom and run them through a structured course designed to help them implement the change

- Develop e-learning and track whether people completed the online curriculum

- Develop knowledge-management systems and repositories

In our experience, none of these alternatives has been successful at producing real, sustained results for large groups of people. Instructor-led training, in any form, is limited by the availability of generally expensive labor. Electronic forms of training, while highly scalable, have not been effective at motivating or sustaining learning. All are costly and none achieves the desired results.

Instructor-led training, in any form, is limited by the availability of generally expensive labor. Electronic forms of training, while highly scalable, have not been effective at motivating or sustaining learning. All are costly and none achieves the desired results.

The High-Performance Buzz

Building momentum is the foundation of scaling, overcoming many barriers and ultimately becoming self-fulfilling. When everyone wants to be part of something special, they become special themselves, and it is contagious. The key to the large-scale change required for the extraordinary organizational performance is to engage enough people fast enough to generate a "buzz" about both the vision and the change process within the organization. Mass excitement about high performance creates mass high performance.

This can be achieved by guiding large numbers of people into the motivating and sustaining processes discussed in previous sections. Participants feel that they have to embrace the vision of high performance and adopt the new attitudes, thinking and behaviors, or be left behind.

Mass Customization for Change

How do you guide hundreds or even thousands of people to join the "buzz?" Creating such mass transformations has historically been one of the biggest challenges for leaders. The theory of mass customization, implemented by IBM in the mid-1990s to improve its manufacturing processes, helps solve this challenge. As discussed previously, the foundation of mass customization is the idea that the central organization responsible for driving a change must be able to mass-produce the change while, at the same time, providing each participant with the capability of adapting the change to his or her specific circumstances. The "mass" component lets the organization realize all the economies of scale, quality consistency, and standards repeatability of mass production. The "customization" component enables each individual to experience the honor and dignity of fair process while adapting the generalized solution to his/her unique situation.

As applied to improving performance, the organization wants to have all the advantages of mass change – the economies of scale, quality and consistency – without creating a rigid bureaucracy. It can be difficult to maintain the delicate balance between too much and too little centralization. Fortunately, there are clear signs that an organization is out of balance.

When a central group tries to change an organization solely from the perspective of creating the mass change, it is invariably seen as excessively bureaucratic. The complaints are always the same:

- We are unique (different, unusual, etc)!

- You don't understand our situation (market, office, etc.)

We are sure you have heard these many times. Each person, locale, office, market wants to be treated uniquely.

Conversely, if an organization tries to treat everyone uniquely, the effort becomes incredibly expensive and loses the value and synergy of a common focus.

Conversely, if an organization tries to treat everyone uniquely, the effort becomes incredibly expensive and loses the value and synergy of a common focus. Economies of scale and standards are legitimately important.

Mass customization gives organizations good guidance in how to maintain this delicate balance.

A System for Mass Customization of Change

How can an organization consistently and easily find this balance? Within the context of our overall approach, use of the positive deviants' wisdom provides the mass component. The customization component is addressed by providing a unique ability to adapt that wisdom to each individual circumstance. Thus, the vision is preserved, but each person comes to see the means of achieving it as uniquely his or her own.

More specifically, by reading the positive deviant content out loud (including the social goals, big steps, principles and practice tasks), discussing them, and, most important, rewriting the core ideas in his/her own language, each participant experiences the underlying drivers of the vision yet translates them into a personal conceptual model and practice exercises. Note that the focus is on the conceptual framing of the change initiative and not just daily actions. This guides each participant to simultaneously align with the positive deviant's ideas and apply them to his or her own situation.

Furthermore, the expectation that people have both the ability to understand the new concepts and appropriately apply them is the single most effective means of increasing people's sense of honor and dignity, which is the foundation of fair process. Everyone is asked to change and grow in a way that communicates a complete belief in their abilities, thereby honoring them.

Focusing (and Limiting) Customization

What happens if someone wants to change the positive deviant content so much that it no longer reflects the original intent? While this is rare, people sometimes disagree with the positive deviants or don't understand them, which leads to inappropriate adaptations.

Here, interaction with the coach plays a significant role. The coaches are responsible for ensuring that the adaptations are consistent with the positive deviant intent. They gently guide the learner back to understanding the positive deviant content with "comparison" questions such as:

"You focused on … . The positive deviants focused on … . What do you think the difference is?"

When the positive deviant content has been developed correctly in Wisdom Discovery, the power of the content dominates the comparison, causing the learners to engage more completely with that content and eventually substitute it for their own conceptual models. It is quite rare for someone to stay permanently outside the mass part of the program.

Coaches and Scaling

You might infer from this that coaches are a potential impediment to scaling. After all, they obviously play a critical role in ensuring the success of the program, a role that is very human-dependent, and therefore limits scaling.

The actual result is quite the opposite. Involving the coaches, and middle management in general, in this program is critical to scaling. In our experience, one of the main reasons most initiatives are unsuccessful is minimal support from middle management.

> In our experience, one of the
> main reasons most initiatives are
> unsuccessful is minimal support
> from middle management.

Too often, middle management is focused so exclusively on just running the business that it doesn't allocate its attention or its people's attention to achieving high performance.

By giving coaches a meaningful role – and in the one-day training on becoming a coach, guiding the coaches to develop insight into the opportunities for their own development – this program positively enlists them in helping the organization achieve its higher purpose. So, paradoxically, energizing the coaches produces complete organizational alignment and is therefore a major asset for scaling.

The Result

Mass customization, especially when supported by a "persuasive technology" (see the next chapter), creates the capability to motivate hundreds or thousands of people to change their attitude, thinking and behavior to align with a key initiative. All of this is accomplished with minimal central direction and control. When a sufficient number of people embrace the change this way and are functioning in the new mode, the change feels as though it were generated from the grassroots of an organization and industry. This leads to fast adoption and the rapid and systematic transformation of large groups. That is something that a leader can well take satisfaction in achieving.

12

Organizational Persuasive Technology

Jocelyn is the worldwide program manager for the deployment of a new customer-demand forecasting methodology at a high-tech company. Accurate demand forecasting is critical because it is the primary data used to meet (or exceed) customer requirements while minimizing inventory costs. In markets that are increasingly volatile, it is extremely difficult to forecast accurately.

This is made more challenging for Jocelyn because, in many cases, the people creating the forecasts are new to the role. In other cases, experienced forecasters must "unlearn" their old behavior patterns and quickly learn completely new attitudes, thought patterns and behaviors in order to keep up with the current market. She has used the methodology presented here over the past year to drive the change she and her company sought.

Making this situation more complicated is the organization's geographic separation. Jocelyn is based near Sacramento, California, and has to drive the adoption of the new forecasting program for:

• 65 people in the United Kingdom

- *25 people in Hong Kong*

- *72 people in Shenzhen, China (just north of Hong Kong)*

- *45 people in Sacramento*

- *5 people in Beijing*

- *70 people in Japan*

Also, each month she has to report on the progress of all of the above to an executive committee responsible for improving forecast accuracy.

How can Jocelyn instill her vision and drive her program, quite literally, around the world while providing clear visibility into progress — all from her desk in Sacramento?

The Importance of Technology

Can you achieve scaling of the type Jocelyn requires without technology? While we think it is theoretically possible, we don't really see how it can be done effectively. The use of Web applications makes it easy for hundreds or thousands of people to connect to a central application simultaneously and at very low cost. This means that many people can be engaged in learning the positive deviant content, reporting progress and tracking at minimal incremental expense. It would be very hard to accomplish this without using the Web, servers and software.

Persuasive Technology

However, the program presented here makes specific demands on how the technology interacts with the user, so it can't be just any technology. A technology to support our approach must effectively gather the positive deviant content, stimulate strong motivation to learn and apply the content, and guide sufficient practice of new behaviors to promote sustained change.

For many people, the very notion of a technology designed to create motivation is something of a disconnect from their view of technology. After all, how in the world can interaction with a software application drive commitment to achieving a greater social good? Can technology really change what people believe and how they function?

In general, this technology "persuades"
by providing end-users with a series
of visual, linguistic and aural cues
that guide them into a particular
interaction with the technology.

Fortunately, as we discussed in Chapter 3, a new category of technology called "persuasive technology" has recently emerged. Persuasive technology is software specifically designed to "change people's attitudes and behaviors," according to Dr. B.J. Fogg at the Stanford University Persuasive Technology Lab. This is exactly what performance-improvement initiatives, programs and projects are designed to do, isn't it?

In general, this technology "persuades" by providing end-users with a series of visual, linguistic and aural cues that guide them into a particular interaction with the technology. For example, the ubiquitous pop-ups on many Web sites that offer opportunities for you to spend your money are a crude version of persuasive technology because they give you a cue that guides your behavior. A more subtle form of persuasive technology is Amazon.com providing you with a list of books purchased by others who purchased the book you are interested in. The technology responds to your initial interest and tries to persuade you to buy additional books.

Organizational Persuasive Technology

As suggested by the preceding examples, until very recently most persuasive technology has been focused on changing consumer behavior, often in rather unsubtle or even offensive ways. We are more interested in a small group of emerging persuasive technologies that are designed to transform organizations, ideally without any of the negative effects.

We have coined the term "organizational persuasive technologies" (OPT) to define this emerging category of persuasive technologies. OPT applications are designed specifically for the complexity of change found in an organizational environment, the need for personal and organizational integrity, and the importance of showing a substantial return on the investment.

Not surprisingly then, we find that the best OPT uses many of the principles and much of the science outlined in this book. For example, many of the on-screen cues used by high-quality OPT are based on the research about fair process and "self-directed neuroplasticity." Similarly, good OPT incorporates mass customization, creating significant economies of scale while allowing extensive personalization. A good OPT application is critical for scaling.

Evaluating OPT

Because OPT is so new, few people know how to evaluate the quality of an OPT application specifically for how it might support our approach.

Here are some of the factors we use to evaluate OPT applications. Focusing first on the impact on the end-user, we ask ourselves whether it:

- Creates a perception for the user of a one-on-one coaching experience

- Provides the user with a structured flow of interaction that carefully builds commitment and knowledge

- Guides people into positive visualization of the content

- Guides people to customize the mass portion of the content (the positive deviant wisdom) to fit their own situation (through reading, feedback and adaptation)

- Creates a schedule for practice that drives long-term learning

- Identifies risks and establishes risk management plans

- Drives the recording of learning and the reflection associated with progress tracking.

More generally, we look for users to show an initial response to the OPT and its positive deviant content in just a few minutes. This response should manifest as a distinct physical change. Users should lean forward, tap the screen, breathe faster, focus their eyes more, and make statements like:

"I never thought of myself this way, but this is a great way to think about myself and my job."

These are strong, observable indicators of high quality OPT because they suggest intense engagement with the positive deviant content.

Similarly, we evaluate how the OPT will work in an organization by asking whether the OPT:

- Provides a structure for the coaches, enabling each coach to be extraordinary

- Summarizes the progress tracking so the organization can provide quick, effective support for the initiative.

Those are the basic characteristics of a fundamentally sound OPT application. When used in support of the methodology presented here, OPT that meets these criteria can drive very consistent and predictable transformational response patterns for large numbers of people very quickly. As such, OPT is a powerful tool for driving change.

Advanced Capabilities

In addition to the criteria above, we often look for more sophisticated capabilities in an OPT application. A great OPT application will also provide capabilities that help overcome the impact of the six-week resistance barrier discussed earlier. Recall that approximately six weeks into a change initiative, there is often resistance to the adoption of the new, desired attitudes and behaviors.

We evaluate OPT's ability to overcome the six-week barrier by asking whether it:

- Generates a series of reminders and prompts that cause people to continuously refresh their commitment to the overall objective

- Encourages people to engage in the practice required to achieve greatness

- Informs a participant's personal and organizational support network, including his or her coach, about progress and problems (which helps generate a supportive organizational "buzz").

In short, we determine whether the OPT helps all participants sustain their focus on the practice required to internalize the vision.

Computer-phobia

Many organizations and individuals will immediately resist even the idea of OPT because of general fears about technology. People have told us that OPT would never work in their organizations because everyone was either computer-phobic or minimally computer-literate. This is a particular concern in lower-technology environments such as retail, construction, quick-service food chains, etc.

Consequently, we also evaluate the ease of use and simplicity of the application. If OPT has all of the above capabilities, but scares people with its complexity, then the organization will still be limited in its ability to scale.

If OPT has all of the above capabilities, but scares people with its complexity, then the organization will still be limited in its ability to scale.

Fortunately, this has not been a significant problem for OPT, particularly applications aligned with our approach. Because of its humble origins trying to sell products and services to general consumers, most OPT has been designed to operate so simply that the end users don't need any training and the coaches need only a few hours. Even people who couldn't type and didn't speak English as a first language were able to quickly and effectively master the use of OPT. Usually, the positive deviant content is so interesting to people that they quickly forget they are working with a technology and focus intensely on the content itself. They blank out the technology and are completely engaged in customizing the content to their own situations. Computer-phobia should not be a problem.

The Result

Can you achieve your leadership moment for an initiative without utilizing organizational persuasive technology? As we said at the beginning of the chapter, while it is theoretically possible to use this approach without technology, it is certainly challenging to achieve sustained impact and mass customization without it.

However, the idea of implementing more software is a discouraging prospect for most of us. None of us wants to go through yet another software learning experience. So, is organizational persuasive technology worth it? Our answer is "absolutely!" Well-designed persuasive technology saves the organization significant time and money.

Section 6

Summing Up

13

A Disruptive Methodology

An organizational development manager at a large insurance company conducted a detailed review of the approach presented here. She concluded that it would drive the changes in her organization faster, more predictably and more completely than she had thought possible. She also concluded that it would scare many people in the organization.

We asked her why she thought it would scare them. She said:

"They may talk about how important it is to have extraordinary performance, but they don't really want to change, even when their jobs depend on it!"

This is a breakthrough methodology. As such, it is different both in its approach to change and in the power it brings to driving change. For many people, using a different approach is uncomfortable. When coupled with the speed and depth it brings to the change process, discomfort can become severe in some cases.

Of course, the very definition of a breakthrough is that it is a significant change, diverging from many prevailing values, business practices and existing thinking. The major strength of a breakthrough is that it creates capabilities that were previously thought impossible. The major weakness is that it challenges the status quo, creating discomfort and resistance.

The major strength of a breakthrough is that it creates capabilities that were previously thought impossible.

How is our approach a breakthrough? It diverges from conventional approaches by:

- Focusing on how to do something "right," looking toward a desirable future rather than concentrating on the past – as occurs in assessments of current state, the foundation for most current performance improvement initiatives. This creates significant saving of both time and resources by creating a positive focus for the transformational work.

- Relying on positive deviants within the organization, rather than expertise outside the organization, particularly consultants. This generates a better, more complete and powerful model of high performance that can be built faster. Use of positive deviance also establishes a better foundation for motivating participation and sustaining the change.

- Employing the most recent research on self-directed neuroplasticity, reducing dependence on classroom instructors and managers as the primary motivators. This facilitates stronger motivation and better retention of the new capabilities.

- Utilizing highly innovative persuasive technologies, rather than less effective e-learning or complex knowledge management systems. This enables scaling of the learning to large numbers faster and more comprehensively than previously thought possible.

If it is so different, what exactly is this methodology? We humans love to put things in categories. How do we categorize this new approach? Is it:

- A training system?

- A knowledge management system?

- A project management system?

- A performance management system?

This approach is, in a sense, all of these and none of these at the same time. It takes the best from each category, as well as several others, and combines them in a completely new way. It trains people, but it is much more than a training system. It certainly captures and utilizes expert knowledge, but it is much more than any conventional knowledge management system. It guides people into making a personal commitment schedule like a project management system, but it is much more than simply scheduling tasks. It manages performance but it is more than performance management.

What is it then? Simply put, it is a high performance means of achieving high performance. The breakthrough successes achieved by this approach are the result of combining the latest findings in several areas of science with the best components of the traditional approaches described above.

The Natural Reaction

Not surprisingly, we often encounter people and organizations that plaintively say:

"This is too much! Give me the old tried and true,
even if it doesn't work."

On one occasion, the chief operating officer of a men's apparel chain even told us:

"I know my current sales training program is not working, but I will
never get in trouble with anyone by doing the same old thing."

As it turned out, the last part of his statement wasn't exactly true. A short while after we spoke with him he was fired because of declining performance in his chain. Maybe you can get in trouble for doing the same old thing – especially when it doesn't work!

His sentiment is quite common, however. We look at this resistance to change from a rather clinical perspective asking a series of questions:

- Does the organization really want to improve performance?

- Does the organization accept the idea that it can't improve performance without changing some things?

- Does the organization recognize that change requires commitment, work and, quite possibly, some discomfort?

These questions elicit interesting reactions. To an amazing degree, we find that people answer "yes" to the first question. Most people really do want high performance. However, many people answer "no" to the second question. That suggests an interesting paradox. People want the benefit of a change without having to change, which brings to mind the famous quote about insanity, often attributed to Albert Einstein :

"There is nothing that is a more certain sign of insanity than to do the same thing over and over and expect the results to be different."

This remains true today: If you want to improve, you must change.

Once you're ready to embrace change and focus on becoming a high performing organization, then several additional questions must be addressed:

- Do you believe that a definition of high performance is essential?

- Do you believe that you must actively motivate people to embrace the goals of high performance in order to be successful?

- Do you believe that you must create sustained high performance (i.e., really change the organization) in order to be successful?

- Do you want high performance throughout your entire organization no matter its size or structure?

Obviously, those are almost rhetorical questions. How can you say "no" to any of them if you really want to be a high performing organization? Of course it is important to have an image of high performance in order to develop specific capabilities. Of course you need to motivate people to change or the change won't occur. Of course you need to sustain the change or all of the previous work is meaningless. Of course you need to get as many people involved as possible. Can you achieve high performance without any of these? Not in our experience. An organization needs all of them to be effective.

The Inherent Conflict

Is it possible to achieve high performance using the current approaches to change? Obviously some companies are consistently high performing using these older methodologies. Why can't your organization achieve the same high performance without using a process like ours? Why can't you just keep using your same training, consultants and knowledge-management systems?

We have found that in addition to more conventional approaches, most high performance companies today have achieved their excellence through one or more of the following:

- Charismatic leadership. They have a leader who is effective at creating motivation and "pushing" his/her vision throughout the organization

- Established culture. They have created, over time (sometimes many, many years), a culture that breeds excellence.

- Luck. Sometimes companies are just in the right place at the right time. They hire the right person, enter the right market, or get the right "boost" when they need it.

In other words, those organizations are considered high perform-ers in spite of their use of traditional methods, not because of them. Simply put, the results obtained by using traditional means of improving organizational performance are unreliable and unpredictable.

Simply put, the results obtained by using traditional means of improving organizational performance are unreliable and unpredictable.

More specifically, Table 13-1 compares traditional approaches with the Strategy to Action approach described here. Those older methodologies don't do very well against the criteria needed to create high performance. Each of the more traditional methods certainly has strengths, but each has key weaknesses as well.

Some patterns become apparent when reviewing this chart. The human-driven alternatives (classroom training and mentoring) can have great impact if the designers, instructors or mentors are quite good. But having that level of consistent quality is relatively rare. In addition and more importantly, they are weak in sustaining and scaling changes. On-going support is usually expensive and scaling is difficult, since they are both constrained by the number of people who can be trained at any one time. In addition, development times can be quite long which can significantly delay initial rollout.

Poor ✔   Good ✔ ✔   Excellent ✔ ✔ ✔

Criteria	Class Training	E-Learning	Book Binders Videos	Mentors	KM Systems	Strategy to Action
Quality of High Performance Model	✔ ✔	✔	✔	✔ ✔	✔	✔ ✔ ✔
Ease of Adaptability	✔ ✔	✔	✔	✔ ✔ ✔	✔	✔ ✔ ✔
Ability to Motivate Participants	✔ ✔	✔	✔	✔ ✔ ✔	✔	✔ ✔ ✔
Ability to Sustain Learning	✔	✔	✔	✔ ✔	✔	✔ ✔ ✔
Ability to Scale Learning	✔	✔ ✔ ✔	✔ ✔	✔	✔ ✔ ✔	✔ ✔ ✔
Speed (strategy to deployment)	✔	✔	✔	✔ ✔	✔	✔ ✔ ✔
Overall Impact On Long Term Performance	✔ ✔	✔	✔	✔ ✔	✔	✔ ✔ ✔

Note: A more detailed table is supplied in Appendix B

Table 13-1: Approaches to Organizational Change

Conversely, e-learning, books, and knowledge management systems are scalable, but generally have low impact because they are weak on the initial content, motivation and sustainability. Also, as with training, development times are lengthy.

In short, none of the traditional approaches to organizational change effectively addresses all of the requirements for achieving a high-performing organization.

This chart also suggests that the ideal approach to creating a high-performance organization is to have the impact and effectiveness of a great mentor, supported by great classroom training for specific skill-building, delivered in a way that can be scaled. That of course is the purpose and design of the methodology discussed here – using the best of each of those in a way that is sustainable and scalable.

Outside Consultants

Notice that we have not included outside consultants in this analysis. Strictly speaking, an outside consultant is not a change methodology, but is more typically someone who brings his or her own methodology into the organization based around one or more of these traditional approaches.

There is no question that outside consultants can provide significant value. The good ones bring extensive experience gained in a diverse range of situations. This can be useful. However, no outside consultant understands your unique situation, culture and environment as well as your positive deviants

---

However, no outside consultant understands your unique situation, culture and environment as well as your positive deviants.

We find that the positive deviants consistently bring better expertise and more focused energy to a change than can be brought in by any outsider.

Surprisingly, people often reject that perspective. It is almost as though they don't trust themselves, their peers or their organization to know and do the right things. Somehow an outside "expert" seems more legitimate.

In our experience, that is rarely the case. The positive deviants are by far the best source of expertise in an organization, and they are a lot less expensive than a consultant too!

Consultants also bring to an organization the ability to conduct an outside assessment. We frequently hear statements like:

How do I know what to fix if I don't
first figure out what's wrong?

Unfortunately, there are many problems with this perspective and with assessments in general. Assessments focus more on what is going wrong than what is going right. From a neuroscience perspective this is completely backward. Remember that recent research tells us neurons that fire together wire together, and that this wiring together comes from repetition. Assessments focus a lot of attention on what's wrong, which creates many repetitions of exactly the wrong capabilities. It is like a golfer who gets up to the ball and thinks, "don't hit it to the left; don't hit it to the left." Do you know what invariably happens? The golfer hits it to the left. The repetitions are wiring the golfer's brain to do exactly the wrong thing. That's why you see professional golfers stand behind the ball and look down the fairway. They are visualizing the "perfect" shot. They are focusing on the "right" thing to do and not on what could go wrong. Focusing on what an organization is doing wrong, is the wrong thing to do.

Similarly, by focusing almost entirely on what needs "fixing," solutions generated from assessment findings are naturally incremental. Framing performance improvements as incremental change, such as "we need to improve customer service," does not generate creative solutions or much energy.

In contrast, directly focusing on how to achieve greatness or excellence concentrates neural activity in positive ways and is more likely to develop superior, energizing solutions. Also, this approach is effectively free and almost instantaneous, particularly when compared with the cost and time required for an assessment.

Finally, organizations that overuse consultants tend to become reliant on them. When they leave (which eventually happens in all cases), the organization quickly reverts to its original state. Consultants may make an organization feel better in the short term (and you will pay for that good feeling), but they have little lasting impact. No matter how great a consultant is (and there certainly are some great ones), they just cannot get you to sustained high performance. You can only get yourself to high performance.

Your Choice

So where does this leave you? In a sense, you have a simple choice. You can either:

- Use the approach described here to achieve predictable high performance;

- Continue to try to achieve high performance with traditional means, which have been shown to cost more while being less effective and largely unsustainable; or

- Stop trying for high performance entirely – in essence, do nothing.

We are now back to the conflict we defined in the opening paragraphs of this chapter. Everyone wants high performance, but doing the work requires significant commitment and it can be scary. The choices above are mutually exclusive. We firmly believe that it is extremely difficult, bordering on impossible, to achieve high performance without doing all of the things included in the methodology described here

---

We firmly believe that it is extremely difficult, bordering on impossible, to achieve high performance without doing all of the things included in the methodology described here.

Ironically, if you do choose to implement this methodology in your organization, the breakthrough aspect of it means that you can actually achieve high performance with less effort and cost, and with greater speed than ever before.

14

Achieving High Performance

We were talking with the vice-president of operations for a 110-store carpet chain. He had two key issues:

- *Some of his stores consistently and substantially outperformed others*

- *He was trying to shift the culture of the stores from "selling carpet" to being an "advisor on flooring for elegance."*

He had been trying to make those changes for a long time, without much success.

As we took him through our methodology he asked many questions, ending with these two:

"Are you telling me that you can do in a few weeks

what I have not been able to do in the past five years?"

When we said, "Yes, we are," he then asked,

"How is that possible?"

We then said, "It is the science. The science creates capabilities that were not possible even a few years ago."

Does This Method Work? (Revisited)

This entire book has been about enabling an organization to achieve that sweet moment when your vision for high performance has been realized. In that moment, people tell us they feel a sense of satisfaction beyond easy description. For many, the realization that they can achieve their vision more quickly and predictably than they ever thought possible is enough for them to embrace the process described here.

For many, the realization that they
can achieve their vision more quickly
and predictably than they ever
thought possible is enough for them to
embrace the process described here.

Others require more than just personal satisfaction. They need to see tangible results from the process. In earlier chapters we showed some of the results obtained from this process. We have described the impact at:

- A high tech manufacturer

- A quick-service restaurant chain

- An auto-parts company

Here is another example from the work we recently did with an insurance company. In this company, it was fairly easy for an agent to write up to 2,000 policies. At that level the agents were making a lot of money without working very hard. Consequently, nearly 70% of the company's agents had achieved that goal, but not many had moved beyond it. Most were stuck at about 2,000 policies. This meant that the company was relying on a tiny percentage of its agents for its continued growth.

In order to meet its growth goals, the company had to break its agents out of the "2,000-policy plateau." That was challenging, because almost everything that was done to reach 2,000 policies had to change. Paper systems had to be computerized, additional staff needed to be hired and trained and, most important, the agents themselves needed to have more motivation to grow.

Using our approach, the company gathered a team of positive deviant agents who had written as many as 10,000 policies and used Wisdom Discovery to develop a set of best practices for how to achieve more growth. Those best practices were then quickly deployed to a test group of 30 agents who were specifically selected because they were complacent at 2,000 policies. The goal was to increase growth beyond the national policy growth rate of 2.9% to a target of 6%.

Within six months, the 30 agents increased their policy count an average of 15%, with the top performers reaching a 25% growth rate – far beyond the target! Even more, every single agent that used our system exceeded the national growth rate.

This is just another of the quantitative results that have been achieved. However, we need to introduce a little cautionary note. Many environments do not have clean, precise impact measures such as those described above. Here are some less precise, but still telling, examples of impact:

- A manufacturing company was able to bring a new management process to the factory floor within six days of conceiving the need for the change (beating our 10-day standard).

- A federal agency was able to reduce training time for key employees from three years to three months.

- After trying for five years, a medium-size construction company was able to implement its groundbreaking integrated architecture and construction process in just four months.

- A financial consultant was able to increase his company's annual revenues substantially, doubling his profits in the process.

This methodology is not just theory. It is actually being applied and the results carefully measured, in numerous companies across many diverse industries.

Looking for the Quick Fix

Even with those successes and the documented speed of this process, we frequently find that people want to shorten it even further or reduce the work involved. They think they can implement just portions of the model. Here are the two most frequent questions we get (and the answers):

1. Can we just do the Wisdom Discovery and provide the content to people with training classes and/or binders?

Yes, but any motivation you generate will be dependent on the quality of the instructor. You will also give up the ability to sustain and scale your solution. Is it worth it to build a great model of high performance and not do the things required to make sure you actually achieve this performance level?

2. Can we skip the Wisdom Discovery, put in the content some other way, and still use the later sections of the model?

Again yes, but the content is not likely to be as good, particularly the articulation of the social objective. This decreases the impact of all of the later stages. In particular, you will give up much of the motivational and sustaining capabilities.

The reality is that the steps in the model, and the underlying science are tightly integrated (Figure 14-1). Each step relies on critical elements of the previous step. The model acts like a single, almost organic whole that delivers an in-depth solution – high performance. As we recently explained to someone, the complete model is itself a high-performance way to achieve high performance.

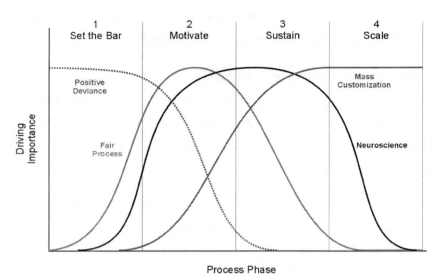

Figure 14-1: Driving Importance of Various Science Areas

Will this Work for Your Organization?

As we have said, this approach has been used in a wide variety of industries for many different performance-improvement initiatives. It has also been used to address a wide variety of specific and unusual needs including:

- **Multi-national, multi-cultural organizations** – This approach has been used in Europe, Japan, China, Malaysia, South America, and the United States. There do not seem to be any language or cultural barriers to its effectiveness.

- **Franchise Operations** – This approach has been used to optimize both franchisee and franchisor performance.

- **Consulting and Training** – This approach has been used to create more impact and revenue for people and organizations already selling expertise.

- **Retiring Knowledge Workers** – This approach has been used to gather and protect the knowledge of experts who are approaching retirement.

In short, this process works for any organization that wants to seriously improve its performance.

Wrapping Up

Is it worth it to employ a methodology like ours?

Remember Heather and Kevin from the introduction? It was definitely worth it for them.

Heather received several promotions and was recognized as one of the key leaders in her company. She was selected out of more than 2,000 people to present her work using this model to a large tradeshow. Kevin also received several promotions and was recruited out of his company to be a private consultant at a huge increase in salary.

We can't guarantee a promotion, but we are confident that you will experience the elation that comes with such an accomplishment and the recognition that comes from being a true leader. So, what are you waiting for? Select an initiative and assemble your positive deviants. Then create your roadmap for success and have at it!

About the Authors

William Seidman, Ph.D.

 Dr. Seidman is a recognized thought leader and expert on how to develop and sustain high performing organizations. In particular, Bill is renowned for understanding the processes required to discover and use expert wisdom.

Bill's doctorate is from Stanford, where he studied management decision-making for eight years. As part of his doctoral dissertation, he developed a groundbreaking technique for analyzing management decision-making. The technique is the core of Strategy to Action methodology and has been recognized by KMWorld, The Innovation Center, IDC and others.

Bill has more than 20 years of experience as a manager in high-technology companies including Hewlett-Packard, Silicon Graphics and Mentor Graphics. As the CEO of Cerebyte, he has led engagements for Hewlett-Packard, Jack in the Box, McGhan Medical, Tektronix, Nike, CVS Pharmacies, Arthur Andersen, Sears, Pricewaterhouse Coopers, Lifetouch, University of Minnesota and many others. Bill can be reached via e-mail at William.Seidman@Cerebyte.com.

Michael McCauley

Michael McCauley is the recognized expert on organizational persuasive technology, intellectual capital management methodologies, Web-based application development and social media usage. Prior to co-founding Cerebyte, Michael spent more than 20 years leading numerous high-performance teams at leading-edge companies such as Compaq Computer, Dell Computer, Motorola, Pacific Bell, Novell, LSI Logic, 3Com, Pacific Gas and Electric, Chevron, DuPont, Xerox, Hewlett-Packard and Microsoft.

He developed the first systematic method for rating the maturity of project management processes within organizations. That pioneering work became the foundation for an extensive study of project management maturity by the Project Management Institute and U.C. Berkeley.

With his extensive background as an engineer and management process consultant, Michael creates persuasive technologies that make systematic and sustainable organizational change possible.

Michael holds a B.S. in engineering from Cal Poly, San Luis Obispo and an MBA in Management from Golden Gate University. He has also been certified by the Project Management Institute as a Project Management Professional. Michael can be reached via e-mail at Michael.McCauley@Cerebyte.com.

Appendix A

Readings in Support of the Underlying Science

Many of the supporting articles below are available on the Cerebyte web site at www.cerebyte.com.

Positive deviance and related topics:

Cameron, Kim, Positive Leadership, (San Francisco, Berrett-Koehler Publishers, 2008)

Pascale, Richard Tanner and Jerry Sternin. "Your Company's Secret Change Agents." Harvard Business Review 83 (May 2005).

Seidman, William and Michael McCauley. "Positive Deviants Rule!" Cutter IT Journal 21, 7 (July 2008): 16-20.

Seidman, William and Michael McCauley. "Harvesting the Experts' Secret Sauce." Performance Improvement 42 (January 2003): 32-39.

Seidman, William and Michael McCauley, "Saving Retiring Knowledge Workers' Secret Sauce," Performance Improvement 44 (September 2005): 34-38.

Fair process and related topics:

Kim, W.Chan and Renee Mauborgne. "Fair Process: Managing in the Knowledge Economy." Harvard Business Review 81 (January 2003).

Seidman, William and Michael McCauley. "Eight Minutes to Performance Improvement." Performance Improvement 42 (July 2006): 23-28.

Neuroscience and related topics:

Restak, Richard. The New Brain. (Rodale, 2003)

Rock, David and Jeffrey Schwartz. "The Neuroscience of Leadership." Strategy + Business (Summer, 2006). http://www.strategy-business.com/press/freearticle/06207

Ross, Philip E. "The Expert Mind." Scientific American.com. July 24, 2006.

Schwartz, Jeffrey and Sharon Begley. The Mind and the Brain. (New York: Regan Books, 2002).

Seidman, William and Michael McCauley. "The Performance Improvement Multiplier." Performance Improvement 42 (October 2003): 33-37.

Mass customization and related topics:

Pine, B. Joseph II, Mass Customization. (Boston: Harvard Business School Press, 1993).

Seidman, William and Michael McCauley. "A Behavioral Approach to Knowledge Management." Cutter IT Journal 17 (December 2004): 11-18.

Persuasive Technology and related topics

Fogg, B. J. Persuasive Technology. (San Franciscon, Morgan Kaufmann Publishers, 2003).

Seidman, William and Michael McCauley. "Organizational Transformation: A New Application of Persuasive Technology." (April 2009). www.Cerebyte.com/articles/Transforming%20Organizations.pdf

Appendix B

Comparison of Organizational Change Approaches

The table on the following pages compares various traditional organizational change methods along with the method presented in this book.

Criteria	Classroom Training	E-Learning	Books, Binders, Videos
Quality of High-Performance model	Good • Relies on instructional designer • Mostly explicit knowledge (official story)	Poor • Relies on instructional designer • Mostly explicit knowledge (official story)	Poor • Relies on developer • Mostly explicit knowledge (official story)
Ease of Adaptability	Good • Good instructor can adapt as needed	Poor • Very difficult and expensive	Poor • Very difficult
Ability to Motivate Participants	Good • Relies on instructor and course design	Poor • Passive media that may or may not be very engaging	Poor • Passive media that is not usually very engaging
Ability to Sustain Learning	Poor • Usually less than 10% long-term retention	Poor • Usually less than 10% long-term retention	Poor • Usually less than 10% long-term retention
Ability to Scale Learning	Poor • Hiring of more instructors	Excellent • Many people can access at once	Good • Many people can access at once
Speed (strategy to deployment)	Poor • Development can takes months • Delivery normally takes place over extended period	Poor • Development and coding usually takes months • Delivery at end user's convenience	Poor • Development and printing usually takes months • Delivery at end user's convenience
Overall Impact on Long-Term Performance	Good • Some quite good, but dependent on instructor quality • Sustainability and scaling difficult.	Poor • Easy to scale, but most is poor quality • Does not motivate participation or sustain learning	Poor • Easy and inexpensive to scale • Do not drive motivation or sustained learning

Mentoring	KM Systems	Strategy-to-Action
Good • Relies on skills of mentor • Relies on mentor making time available	Poor • Inconsistent • Mostly explicit knowledge (official story	Excellent • Relies on highly respected positive deviants • Obtains their expert "wisdom." (real story)
Excellent • Good mentor can adapt as needed	Poor • Very difficult	Excellent • Each coachee adapts wisdom to fit his/her needs
Excellent • Relies on skills of mentor • Consistency difficult	Poor • Passive media that is not very engaging	Excellent • Fair process create engagement • Positive visualization motivates
Good • Relies on follow-up by mentoring	Poor • No mechanism for sustaining learning	Excellent • Uses neuroscience to sustain learning • Uses coaches to sustain learning engagement
Poor • Difficult to get good mentors	Excellent • Many people can access at once	Excellent • Many people can access at once. • Uses persuasive technology
Good • Mentor can usually start quickly • Depends on mentor providing time needed	Poor • Development and population of system usually takes months • Delivery at end user's convenience	Excellent • Extremely fast; can be less than 10 days • Quick to deploy through persuasive technology
Good • Dependent on mentor quality and availability • Sustainability and scaling difficult	Poor • Easy to scale, but most is poor quality • Does not motivate participation or sustain learning	Excellent • Excels on all characteristics needed for high performance

153

Appendix C

Glossary of Terms

Affirmation. A positive declaration about oneself or another person. See Positive visualization, Visualization.

Area of expertise. That subject or skill for which a person has exhibited greater knowledge and success than the average person.

Attention-allocation process. The functions in the brain used to screen sensory inputs and direct and focus mental attention.

Big steps. Major phases of work that build toward achieving a specified objective.

Brainwashing. Persuasion through the use of propaganda or aggressive salesmanship rather than the use of facts and analysis.

Buzz. A feeling of intense enthusiasm, excitement or exhilaration.

Coachee. Someone being coached or mentored by a person trained in a particular topic or process.

Cognitive process. The processes in our brain that intellectually analyze, evaluate and act on information. Also known as "thought processes."

Conscious competence. The state of knowing that you have expertise in a particular area.

Content coaching. The process for guiding a learner to understand and use a particular body of knowledge.

Disruptive methodology. Any process or method that is designed to change the status quo in an organization.

E-Learning. Electronic technology designed to provide users with learning experience.

Engagement. A learner or participant in a change becoming emotionally involved. See Ownership.

Facilitator. Someone who helps to bring about a group outcome by providing indirect or unobtrusive assistance, guidance or supervision.

Fair process. Processes used during a change that are perceived as open and honest. Also known as "procedural justice."

Fire-hose training. A structured session in which massive amounts of content are dumped on participants in a short time.

Fortitude. Courage and commitment, particularly in the face of adversity.

IDC. Interactive Data Corporation, a company specializing in market intelligence, data mining and trend analysis.

Ideal new person. A role played by the facilitator in a Wisdom Discovery Workshop. In this role, the facilitator positions himself/herself as intelligent, competent and motivated, but with very little experience in how to be successful.

Initiative. Any formally defined effort to create change within an organization.

Instant engagement. The ability to very quickly encourage a coachee to relate to the information presented.

Internal experts. Those people within the organization who consistently perform at a level above the group norm. See Positive deviant, Top performers.

Inventory shrink. The difference between the amount of inventory a location should have and the amount it actually has. It is an unwanted or unplanned loss of inventory that is normally a result of miscounts and/or theft.

KMWorld. An annual conference focused on the latest developments in content, document and knowledge management.

Knowledge management. The attempt by an organization to identify, create, catalog, distribute and enable the adoption of insights and experiences.

Knowledge-management system. A place, usually a database accessible via the Internet or company intranet, where the cumulative knowledge of the organization is held and made available.

Knowledge transfer. The absorption and application of new knowledge from either another person or information source to a learner.

Legitimacy. The state of being considered to be reasonable and acceptable.

Leverage. Gaining extra benefit from an action or offering.

Long-term retention. The assimilation of a new attitude, behavior or skill so that it becomes "unconsciously competent" and is present indefinitely.

Mass customization. A system for balancing the need to have centralized economies of scale, quality standards, and consistency with the need to adapt to each individual. Term initially coined by B. Joseph Pine II in the 1990s.

Mental map. A personal picture of a situation or set of relationships.

Mental model. Same as mental map.

Mentoring. A wise and loyal advising relationship.

Metrics. Systematic, numerical measures of an organization's accomplishments over time.

Network. The system of personal relationships among people.

Neural pathways. The connections between neurons that form into structures

Neuron. The basic building block of the brain. Neurons are tiny spark-plug-like pieces of the brain that "fire" the charge that produces thoughts.

Neuroplasticity. The ability of the brain to create new neural pathways; i.e., to think new thoughts and create new behaviors.

Neuroscience. The study of brain function.

Neuroscience of learning. The study of how neurons form new neural pathways that result in new learning.

Neurotransmitters. Chemicals released in the brain that carry specific information.

Obsessive compulsive disorder (OCD). A mental disorder character-ized by intrusive thoughts that produce anxiety, repetitive behaviors aimed at reducing anxiety, or combinations of both.

Official story. A formalized version of reality that represents the accepted perspective in the organization. Typical of what an organiza-tion might write in a brochure or press release. See Real story, Tribal wisdom.

Organizational persuasive technology. Any interactive technology that is designed to promote significant change in organizations. A focused subset of persuasive technologies. Term first coined by Cerebyte.

Ownership. When an individual takes responsibility for learning. See Engagement.

Peer. Someone within the organization who is seen as an equal, in terms of intellect, experience and success.

Perception of legitimacy. The characteristic of a process that is seen as fair, unbiased, and in keeping with established community norms.

Personal network. That group of people with which a person has regular and positive connection, and on which that person can rely for assistance in resolving complex issues or providing emotional support.

Persuasive technology. Any interactive technology that is designed to change peoples' attitudes and/or behaviors. Term first coined by B.J. Fogg.

Positive deviance. An observed departure from group norm behavior, in a direction that benefits the individual members and the group as a whole, by one subgroup of people.

Positive deviant. Anyone who, with the same resources and circumstances as everyone else, is consistently and significantly more successful than the norm. Term first coined by Richard Pascale and Jerry Sternin. See Internal Expert, Top Performers.

Positive visualization. Mentally picturing a successful situation or a successful performance of a function. See Affirmation, Visualization.

Problem-detection mechanism. The ability to identify potential problem situations from specific cues.

Program. Several related projects, often combined with the intention of systematically improving an organization's performance.

Project. A temporary endeavor, having a defined beginning and end, undertaken to meet particular goals and objectives, usually to bring about beneficial change or added value.

Project management. The discipline of planning, organizing and managing resources to bring about the successful completion of specific project goals and objectives.

Read, feedback, adapt. A method first defined by Cerebyte in which a person is asked to read the positive deviant's real story, feed it back in his or her own words, and then adapt it to his or her unique situation.

Real story. A version of reality that more closely reflects what is actually done by real people. It is normally stated using more colloquial terms with a less formal syntax, and is bursting with energy, vision and passion. See Official story, Tribal wisdom.

Risk. Anything that has the potential to delay or stop an initiative, program or project.

Safe opportunity. A place and time where a new skill, process or method can be tried with little risk of impacting an ongoing initiative, program or project.

Scale. Applying a process or solution that has been successful with a limited number of people to large numbers of people throughout an organization.

Secret sauce. The wisdom of positive deviants that enables them to consistently outperform others. This wisdom is often so ingrained in the way they work that they don't recognize it as anything special.

Self-directed neuroplasticity. Using one portion of the brain, usually the prefrontal cortex, to guide the creation of neural pathways associated with new learning in other portions of the brain.

Set the bar. Creation and publicizing of a clear comprehensive definition of what high performance means to the organization.

Six-week barrier. The point in most attempts to create personal change at which individuals tend to slip back into their previous behavior. This point normally occurs approximately six weeks after the change is initiated.

Slow-drip process. Any process that is designed to create small, incremental changes that build on each other over time to create fundamental change in the organization.

Stanford Persuasive Technology Lab. A research facility established to study and further the field of persuasive technology.

Sustain. Complete internalization of new attitudes, cognitive processes and behavioral patterns such that they are used unconsciously and indefinitely.

Top performers. Those people in any organization who consistently perform at a level above the group norm. See Internal Experts, Positive deviant.

Tribal wisdom. Unarticulated, but widely understood and accepted, knowledge about how to perform certain functions in the organization. See Real story.

Unconscious competence. The state of having no, or very little, recognition that you exhibit expertise in a particular area.

Visualization. Creating a mental picture of an event or capability. See Affirmation, Positive visualization.

Wisdom. Subtle knowledge that goes beyond basic understanding and reflects key learnings about how to perform critical functions.

Wisdom Discovery. A structured process for systematically and efficiently uncovering and gathering wisdom.

Wisdom transfer. A process for enabling new learners to understand and apply wisdom.

Congratulations on taking the first step in transforming your organization!

We have a number of products and services designed to help you move beyond the book and make a lasting change in your organization.

Strategy to Action Quick Start Package

This value-priced package includes everything you'll need to improve performance in your organization. It guides you to discover your organization's wisdom, create a success roadmap and begin coaching your teams.

Strategy to Action "How To" Seminar

In these exciting sessions an expert will guide you through the process step by step. These sessions provide you with techniques that go beyond the book and coach you to apply our approach to your unique situation.

Strategy to Action Onsite Solutions

Invite our experts into your organization. We will help you quickly develop and deploy a solution that produces extraordinary performance almost immediately.

See how these and other Strategy to Action products can work for you by visiting **www.Cerebyte.com**

To receive an added bonus, enter "BOOK" as the special offer code when ordering any of our products!

We love hearing about your successes too! E-mail your stories to us at STA@Cerebyte.com.

We promise – if you send it, we will read it!

TreeNeutral™

LaVergne, TN USA
17 March 2011
220588LV00002B/108/P